ALA Editions • **SPECIAL REPORTS**

DOING SOCIAL MEDIA SO IT MATTERS

A LIBRARIAN'S GUIDE

LAURA SOLOMON

AMERICAN LIBRARY ASSOCIATION
Chicago   2011

Laura Solomon is library services manager for the Ohio Public Information Network and former web applications supervisor for the Cleveland Public Library. She has been doing web development and design and conducting classes in public libraries and as an independent consultant for more than a decade. In 2009, the Ohio Library Council recognized her for her role in saving more than $147 million of public library funding by utilizing her expertise in social media tools. She was tapped as one of *Library Journal*'s "Movers and Shakers" for 2010. She earned her MLS from Kent State and was awarded her MCIW (Master Certified Internet Webmaster) in 2004. Visit her blog at www. meanlaura.com.

Printed in the United States of America

15 14 13 12 11   5 4 3 2 1

While extensive effort has gone into ensuring the reliability of the information in this book, the publisher makes no warranty, express or implied, with respect to the material contained herein.

Note that any URLs referenced in this volume, which were valid at the time of first print publication, may have changed prior to electronic publication.

ISBN: 978-0-8389-1067-2

Library of Congress Cataloging-in-Publication Data
Solomon, Laura, 1967–
    Doing social media so it matters : a librarian's guide / Laura Solomon.
        p.   cm. -- (ALA Editions special report)
    Includes bibliographical references and index.
    ISBN 978-0-8389-1067-2 (alk. paper)
    1. Online social networks--Library applications. 2. Social media. 3. Libraries and community. I. Title.
    Z674.75.S63S65 2011
        302.30285--dc22   2010034319

Series cover design by Casey Bayer.
Series text design in Palatino Linotype and Avenir by Karen Sheets de Gracia.

♾ This paper meets the requirements of ANSI/NISO Z39.48-1992 (Permanence of Paper).

ALA Editions also publishes its books in a variety of electronic formats. For more information, visit the ALA Store at www.alastore.ala.org and select eEditions.

CONTENTS

Social media is like teen sex. Everyone wants to do it. Nobody knows how.
When it's finally done there's surprise it's not better.

—AVINASH KAUSHIK, ANALYTICS EVANGELIST

PROOF OF CONCEPT

On June 19, 2009, at approximately 4 p.m., the world changed for public libraries in Ohio. The Ohio governor made an unanticipated announcement, proposing a 50 percent cut to funding for public libraries. Previous to the announcement, Ohio was known as having some of the best public libraries in the nation. Considering that the vast majority of public libraries in the state received a good amount of their operating budgets from the state, this proposal would have decimated, or even closed, many of Ohio's libraries.

If the future existence of your institution is in doubt, what do you do? You do what library supporters in Ohio did: you mobilize. Many libraries mobilized their patrons, using their existing patron databases to send urgent e-mails asking them to call their legislators. Some libraries set up dedicated computers where patrons could send messages directly to the governor and the local representative. Others posted signs on their doors, stating their library would be permanently closed if the funding cut went through. These methods were invaluable in getting the word out.

Still other supporters turned to social media, which had the potential of reaching Ohio residents who were not active patrons of their local libraries. These channels moved a great deal faster than almost any traditional form of communication and helped to mobilize tens of thousands of people who might otherwise not have been aware of the crisis.

Within an hour of the governor's announcement, the story was on Twitter. I created a Twitter hash tag (a way to categorize Twitter messages), #saveohiolibraries. The conversation collated around the hash tag, and it became one of the top forty most popular topics on Twitter. A Facebook group, Save Ohio Libraries, was started. It had over 50,000 members in less than three weeks. Mandy Knapp, a librarian from Worthington Libraries, began a website at www.saveohiolibraries.com, where she tracked the latest developments on the issue and where people could leave their own stories of why they needed their library. (And there were many stories!) Some patrons even put videos in support of libraries on YouTube. The social media movement was strong enough to garner support from such notables as author Neil Gaiman and celebrity blogger Perez Hilton. The Ohio library funding crisis had hit the national stage.

Between social media and other efforts put forth by libraries and their supporters, the Save Ohio Libraries movement made a huge impact at the State Capitol. Thousands of phone calls were made by patrons on their libraries' behalf, forcing state officials to add additional staff to handle them. Most legislators received between 37,000 and 45,000 e-mails in a one-week period, resulting in such a volume that an automatic response was put on the servers to try and keep the electronic traffic moving. Legislators commented to Lynda Murray, the director of government and legal services for the Ohio Library Council, that they had never seen anything like it at the Capitol.[1]

Although it was not possible to save all of the funds for Ohio's public libraries from the chopping block, a huge reduction in cutbacks was made; more than $147 million in state funding was saved, preventing the complete devastation of Ohio's nationally known libraries. As of this writing, despite the outpouring of support from Ohio's residents, many libraries are still struggling with the financial cuts. But things would have been much worse if the governor's proposal had come to full fruition.

IT'S NOT THE TOOL, IT'S THE WIELDER

Without social media, the reach of the campaign would have been more limited and much less effective. However, what many fail to understand is that social media doesn't just "happen." In our case, the social media efforts were primarily managed by a few people who were already very active in social networks and knew how to optimize their presence. These people understood core principles that make using these networks worth the work. Without these individuals, it's very likely that Save Ohio Libraries would not have had the impact in these online communities that it did. Many librarians and libraries simply did not have a presence in social media, or at least one that was influential enough to have any effect.

Many libraries do not understand that using social media successfully takes more than just having an account. Social media is a lot like the strategy game Othello. It's incredibly easy to learn but can take a long time to master. However, the minute-to-minute pace of social media does not allow for a long learning curve before claiming mastery. Many libraries take this to mean they should jump into the roaring river of online interaction, but by doing so they miss key concepts of how best to utilize the incredible tool at their fingertips. They waste time, resources, and opportunities to connect with the very people they want and need to reach.

Unlike traditional media, social media has few barriers. It's no longer a question of budget or acquiring the necessary tools; the vast majority of social media applications are free, and participating in social media is far easier than trying to produce a television commercial or print advertisement. The real need is for experienced social media staff in an arena where many mistakenly assume that having the tool is equivalent to having the expertise.

This book is my attempt not only to answer common questions libraries have about using social media but also to explain and demonstrate how libraries can be doing social media more effectively. There are many ways for libraries to enter the social media space, and there are pitfalls along the way; I know, I've seen almost all of them.

It's time to step up to your computer and to learn how to do social media so it *matters*.

NOTE

1. Lynda Murray, e-mail message to author, January 8, 2010.

GETTING A (BETTER) GRIP ON SOCIAL MEDIA

> The world, as it was, no longer is.
>
> —ERIK QUALMAN, AUTHOR OF *SOCIALNOMICS*

THE TOOLS ARE EPHEMERAL

When it comes to discussing anything online, it's hard to argue with the fact that change is constant. How often have you or your coworkers complained that keeping up with everything new on the Web is nearly impossible? There's no doubt that the frenetic pace of online innovations can be daunting. Nevertheless, the pace is not likely to slow. Websites come and go as fast as the social media tools that empower them.

It's not hard to understand that *all* of the current social media tools are, at best, ephemeral. Accepting this idea of constant and immediate change may be hard for libraries, which historically act to preserve information. At the time of this writing, the popularity of MySpace is declining, and Facebook usage is expanding. What's popular today may be irrelevant tomorrow. Twitter may be replaced by something completely different a year from now. In order to be successful in online communities, libraries need to accept this fast pace of change and begin to move with it.

Unfortunately, some shortsighted individuals misconstrue the changing nature of online tools to mean that social media is a fad or something that libraries should avoid entirely. One of the most common questions I hear is, How do I convince my director that social media is important? To help answer that, I'll be introducing some methods to make your efforts more effective.

BOTTOM LINE

Social media sites will change. Concepts will not. Be flexible.

UNDERSTANDING THE LIBRARY'S PLACE IN SOCIAL MEDIA

Librarians may know about the various social media tools and may even teach their patrons how to use them. They may also have some vague idea about using them to promote programs or collections. Most, however, are truly stymied when it comes to understanding how best to use these tools to their benefit. Even more critically, they may fail to understand basic social media concepts, such as how to build trust and reciprocity (social capital), resulting in the library being effectively irrelevant in a particular online community.

It's easy to get a free account on any of the hundreds of social media sites that currently exist, but social media is not about coverage or even necessarily about numbers. It's about making *connections*. That might seem like a touchy-feely way to gauge its value, especially if you're an administrator, but part of learning to handle social media interaction appropriately is to understand that numbers are not the primary consideration. It's true that metrics are something that should be tracked as part of a library's social media work, but social media's goals are quite different from those of traditional advertising media. In fact, I would argue that social media isn't particularly effective for pure advertising. So why participate in a social media community at all?

Simply using the tools to proclaim, "Come to our library's cool program!" won't fly online. Social media is not a one-way broadcast; it can act as a unique bridge that has never been available to libraries before. Social media can do something no other medium can: directly engage and connect our patrons—to the library and to each other. Knowing how to use Facebook, Twitter, MySpace, or the next "it" social media site is just the beginning. Effective social media takes some thought, a lot of time, and, yes, some careful planning. Until you unlock the potential of online social media, it might seem that it is just a stream of consciousness of the masses and, as a communication method, largely pointless.

Librarians often envision the role of the library as a community center. Social media allows them to put this philosophy directly into practice. Think carefully about what the word *community* connotes: a place where various people communicate and interact with one another. If a library uses social media only as a broadcast medium to get the word out, it is not participating in a community but rather using a version of a bullhorn to promote itself to a crowd.

When a library involves itself in social media, it first and foremost has to understand that it's going to be expected to *interact*. To do otherwise is to fail. Let me say that again: To do otherwise is to fail. By failing to participate in conversations and relationships, the library is essentially declaring that it will simply maintain its traditional role as a depository of knowledge.

Libraries are for the people and of the people, to borrow a phrase. Social media is no different. In other words, even though a library is an organizational entity, once it enters the social realm it is perceived as a *person* and will need to act and speak accordingly.

BOTTOM LINE
Interact with people in social media, or risk becoming irrelevant.

LETTING GO OF THE MESSAGE

The successful use of social media requires companies and organizations to "let go of the message." This means that there has to be an inherent understanding on the part of the institution that the staff in charge of public relations no longer has control over what is said about the organization. In many cases, an organization's social networks may act as an informal PR department. For better or for worse, many conversations are happening about businesses (and libraries) online, and these interchanges are not controlled by any "official" entity.

Library administrators have to understand that *patrons* now control the message. This can be even harder yet to comprehend in the context of social media. There is no longer a one-to-many broadcast model for a message. Now, each person participating in a social media site's service constitutes a node on a network that serves many-to-many communication. There is no "official" voice or moderator. Theoretically, all participants have equal standing in these communities, regardless of what positions they might hold in the offline world. This means that people who don't work for your library have as much (some might say more) say as the library does as to what gets said about it.

There is also a tendency for administrators to think only of what they perceive to be "worst case scenarios": What happens if someone makes a negative comment? What happens if the library gets a bad review? The fact is, people have always had not-so-flattering things to say about libraries. The channels for *hearing* those comments, however, were not so wide open or publicly accessible as they now are. This is our twenty-first-century reality: conversations have moved to the online realm and have, therefore, broadened the scope of their audiences. It's likely that the possible size of the audience and the speed at which news can travel via social media are what makes many administrators nervous about embracing it.

Although it's possible that negative commentary will have repeated airings, it's crucial to remember that, under most circumstances, the number of positive remarks will almost always outweigh the negative ones. People want to take ownership of the library's "brand" and want to be able to brag about it, just as they likely do with organizations they are a part of or products or performers they admire.

Bluntly speaking, there is no practical way to control what is or is not said about a library. Libraries that choose to participate in social networks have to internalize this truth. Patrons are no longer just at the receiving end of communications. Patrons now receive *and* send. Some will inevitably say something the library won't agree with; this is the nature of conversation after all. Just keep in mind that social media involvement allows the library to build one-to-one relationships with patrons that can result in more loyalty and possibly advocacy later on.

BOTTOM LINE

Giving up control is hard, but the worst case scenario rarely happens.
Even if it does, it is far outweighed by the potential reach
a library can have via social media.

GETTING ADMINISTRATIVE BUY-IN

Social media might be old hat to you. Maybe you already participate in a social networking site and want to know how to maximize your time in these conversations. Or, perhaps you're in the all-too-common position of having to convince a library administrator that social media is not a fad or a waste of time. In libraries, knowing how to do social media well isn't enough; you also need a social media foundation that is determined by two factors:

1. Competency of the staff actually in charge of the social media
    presence of the library
2. Amount of support provided by the library's administration for social
    media

This is an unfortunate reality for library staff who may have the expertise but not the backing. Social media efforts will likely end in failure without a director's buy-in. At some point, no matter how adept you might be at navigating the social media terrain, you are going to need backup. How will your administration expect you to handle negative comments? How does the director want questions answered that come in via social networks? At the very least, you will need to invest time in building social capital. How much time will your director support?

The first step, of course, is to show that social media has a direct benefit for your library. Administrators can often be industry-insular; in other words, if the staff cannot point directly to another library where a social media endeavor has already been a success, administrators may be reluctant to consider anything else as a legitimate. Also, much of the library profession tends to be traditional in its approach, and administrators can be inherently reluctant to examine strategies from other types of organizations. This can be very self-limiting and rarely leads to real innovation or change.

I am often asked for specific examples of libraries using social media well, and I seldom can cite any. More often, I point to other types of nonprofits or even large corporations that "get it." "Getting it" doesn't mean jumping on the Web 2.0 bandwagon. What it does mean is that these organizations or companies understand that online communication has moved beyond just transmitting a message to a largely receptive audience. Successful social media means that the organization is ready to have two-way conversations online, even if they are negative or uncomfortable. The organization understands that it is involved in building a long-term relationship, not just in completing a quick, anonymous transaction. Companies such as Dell and Zappos.com are famous for their customer relations via social media channels, primarily because they engage directly and consistently with their customers online and under public scrutiny.

Not every social media tool is for every person or every library; some libraries may not even have a demographic that uses this type of communication yet. However, for those libraries that are aware their patrons are out there on social networks, it's critical that they also understand how social media will enhance the library experience. Those patrons have expectations for the members of their online communities. These patrons want their social media connections to act like real people, talk like real people, and not always put themselves first. If your library's director will not allow you to act in accordance with those expectations, it's likely that your future efforts will be rejected.

SO WHAT CAN YOU DO?

How do you convince the reluctant director? There's no magic wand here, but the following sections present some avenues to explore.

Education

An education campaign has to be part of your exertions; facts are important.

Put Information in Front of Them
Find brief, entertaining articles or blog posts that not only explain social media but also showcase examples of how social media provided a concrete benefit. Print them out and send them to the director with a sticky note: "Hi, thought you would find this interesting." Printing something out shows more effort on your part and is less likely to be totally ignored than an e-mail. The sticky note gives it a more personal touch, too. Be sure to tell them you'll follow up so they know you expect them to glance at it.

Tell Stories
I find myself telling personal stories when I'm explaining social media. Anecdotes provide a human perspective and make interesting hooks for people new to the concepts. (After all, social media is all about people.) I often tell the story of how I

was introduced to Twitter: upon first inspection, I honestly thought it was the dumbest online tool I'd ever seen. Once I saw it in use as a way to have informative conversations during conference sessions (a conference backchannel) though, the light bulb went on, and now I can't live without it. I also tell stories about how other aspects of my life have been affected by social media. My husband and I reconnected with the best man from our wedding because someone I met at a conference started following me on Twitter. I have a friend who met his wife via a virtual world. This kind of thing happens all the time. Social media is making the world smaller, and people are connecting to one another in new ways. Show the personal impact to bring your point home.

Highlight the Facts to Diminish the Fears

Does your administrator believe no one will want to interact with a library? A study published by eMarketer in 2009, "Social Network Marketing Expands Sphere," showed that more than half of the users of social networks have followed or become a fan of a brand online.[1] If someone is going to become a fan of local restaurants on Facebook, they may also want to be a fan of their library. Is the director afraid that people will say negative things? The same study found that users are much more likely to rave than to rant. For nearly every concern, there are facts, figures, and case studies to address it. Check the bibliography for some resources to help you.

Downplay the Tech

This is not about any cool technologies or your enthusiasm for them. Your director is looking at the big picture. Ultimately, it will come down to whether or not social media is good for the library. Technology becomes less relevant than what the library potentially will get out of it: more potential support at levy time and advocates who will call their representative when funding comes under fire. These deliverables may mean more to an administrator than the technology.

Explain What Happens If an Outsider Hijacks the Library's Name

The practice of taking someone/something else's name online is called *brandjacking*, and even if your library isn't in social media space, someone could grab its name. If that were to happen, it would be incredibly difficult to shut down the culprit. Meanwhile, there's no knowing what damage might have been done to the library's reputation. Claiming an identity on social networks is just as important as buying domain names for your library. Even if your director isn't eager to start posting status updates, the library should at least go through the steps of claiming the library's name by setting up accounts on popular networks. Once your library is there, it will likely start accumulating followers. At that point, you can emphasize to your administration that these fans are expecting some communication.

Keeping Up with the Joneses

If your director is a very competitive person, chances are good he or she will want to investigate what other libraries are doing. Find libraries in your region or state that are already engaged in social media. Specifically, make an effort to find examples where the library is interacting directly with patrons and not just broadcasting promotions such as program announcements. Look for the libraries that are actually engaging in conversations in a public online forum with their patrons. These libraries are your library's role models. Send links or printouts to members of your administration with a brief note: "Look at what Example Library does. They're talking directly with their patrons online!" Your competitive director will likely be intrigued.

Show What's Already Out There

Search Google and all of the major social networks for your library's name. Check Yelp for reviews about your library, and location-based services such as FourSquare to see if anyone has posted any tips about your branches. Collate whatever you find and send it to the director. If your search is especially fruitful, you'll also turn up some not-so-flattering things as well as positive or neutral ones. Why is this kind of feedback a good thing? Because it clearly shows you can't effectively respond unless you're in the space with the person who posted it. If you don't find any negative items, it still is clear proof that people *are* talking about the library in social media spaces. The library needs to be in that social media space to listen and connect.

Recommend Something Else

If you've been pushing Twitter without results, consider moving to a push for Facebook. It could be the director has specific objections to a particular tool rather than to social media as a whole.

Hand Holding

In some cases, the administrator you are seeking to convince may be interested but not sure where to start. Being overwhelmed with all of the choices is not uncommon. Try to remember what it was like when you were a complete newbie and what you wished someone had done for you then.

Invite Them

Granted, it might be a bit awkward to "friend" your director on Facebook. But what about something like Twitter? Or LinkedIn? Most social media sites provide members with ways to invite nonmembers to join. Remember, it's a lot like a party—it's easier to go there if you already know someone. Again, follow-up is crucial to success. If your director doesn't respond right away, be sure to ask if he or she received the invitation.

Sit Down and Help Them

Sometimes, you just need to *be* there. Offer to spend an hour walking the director through the social network of choice and help in finding colleagues to connect with that you both already know. Show how to add apps to Facebook or LinkedIn accounts. Just be sure not to present too much information too fast.

Do Something Concrete

Sometimes, the best way to get buy-in is to show that using a social media tool will do something very specific. Look for something that will interest your library's administration, such as creating video tutorials for using the online catalog or getting feedback on a new service. But beware the "when you have a hammer, every problem looks like a nail" approach; don't let your enthusiasm for social media become a solution in search of a problem.

In-House Training

When I was in school, I always enjoyed the opportunities to go beyond the typical take-a-test/write-a-report assignment model. If you're training library staff, ask them to show what they learned by writing a blog post or making a quick video, or even by creating a photo slideshow that's posted to a site like Flickr or Picasa. Give them latitude to do something creative that also makes use of online tools and that they can share with the rest of the staff.

Conferences

No library can afford to send everyone to every conference. Introduce your director (and any attending staff) to Twitter hash tags. The staff going to the conference can send tweets with relevant points, marked with the hashtag for the conference; the director and other interested staff can follow them and other conference-goers on Twitter. By following the hash tag, people from your library will get a nearly real-time sense of what's happening at the conference, and more important, they'll also connect in a new way with their coworkers.

New Initiatives

Is your library about to do something new on a large scale? Self-check machines? Print management? New ILS? Whatever it is, an internal blog to track announcements, information, and feedback may be perfect for introducing new social media tools. It may also reduce the need for formal training time down the road. Not every blog needs to be forever; some have a limited lifespan or purpose. A blog (with comments turned on!) is a good way to experiment internally with some of the "feel" of social media. You also could open up the blog and comments to the public at large and get patron feedback on the new service.

BOTTOM LINE

Everyone has an "Aha!" moment when experimenting with new social media. I did with Twitter. It may be your director's aha is yet to come. Keep sending relevant search results and articles. Hang in there and be an advocate for social media, but be aware that people may be turned off if you become too zealous. Keep the enthusiasm but focus on facts.
Getting buy-in from your library's administration may be challenging at first. Chip away at resistance, try different methods, but don't give up.

Getting Staff Buy-in

You may think you're ready to begin once you've been given the green light from your library's administrator. You'd be at least partially correct; getting administrative approval *is* absolutely essential. However, getting buy-in doesn't end with your library's director. Although it is possible to run a successful social media campaign without the approval of one's colleagues, it is considerably more difficult.

Coworkers who don't understand social media or the library's reason for wanting to engage in it can not only make your job harder but also damage your efforts. Library staff with negative attitudes can undermine you by refusing to provide needed content, creating delays, spreading rumors or gossip, or ignoring the library's social media policy. These staff become obstacles that you have to work around rather than sources of support.

How do you bring these staff members on board with the library's social media ventures? Fortunately, all of the methods you may have used with your library's director are just as applicable to other staff. Some of the methods described in the previous section may work better than others, depending on the person you're working with. Just as with your administrator, you may need to try different approaches to get the support you need. Following are some additional things to consider when getting backing from your colleagues.

One Size Does Not Fit All

Consider each staff person separately. It's unlikely that one person's objections to social media involvement are identical to someone else's. Find out what each individual cares about and address your efforts to those aspects. Are they worried that it will somehow add to their workload? Do they not understand the usefulness of Twitter or think that Facebook is still only for college students? Getting buy-in means proving to reluctant staff that social media is not only relevant to the library's needs but also to their individual needs and concerns. Make sure you have the data or policies readily available to back you up.

Never Assume

Many people who are resistant to social media may only have *heard* of some of the social media sites like Facebook or Twitter and may not have actually used them. Or, if they have tried them, they may have only used a site briefly and not understood that the benefits come after long-term participation. Don't assume that everyone is on a social site like Facebook and understands terms such as "friending," "apps," or "wall." By explaining site-specific terms and customs, you increase the chances of selling the benefits to staff.

Training Can Make a Significant Difference

In addition to educating staff individually, group training can help break down resistance. One of the most successful projects for doing this has been the 23 Things project, originally created by Helene Blowers and launched with the staff of the Public Library of Charlotte and Mecklenburg County in North Carolina.[2] The 23 Things project is a discovery-learning program that helps staff become comfortable with social media technologies by asking them to try different online tools. It has become very popular in the United States and internationally as a way to train staff in the basics of using social media. Hands-on experience can bridge many gaps in understanding.

Ensure That Staff Has Time to Learn before Social Media Is Rolled Out to the Public

Just as with any new initiative or resource at your library, your staff members will feel more secure if they see it in action before their patrons do. Even if they are not the ones doing the posting, seeing social media in action (as with the 23 Things program) can increase their comfort level with how social media works.

BOTTOM LINE

Staff buy-in isn't as critical as administrative buy-in, but not having it can make a social media coordinator's job a lot harder. Make a serious effort to educate and alleviate fears with information and hands-on training.

NOTES

1. "Social Network Marketing Expands Sphere," eMartketer, 2009, www.emarketer.com/Article.aspx?R=1007252.
2. Helene Blowers, "Learning 2.0," 2006, http://plcmcl2-about.blogspot.com.

2

GETTING STARTED

Instead of researching the best ways to engage, many businesses create accounts across multiple social networks and publish content without a plan or purpose. However, businesses that conduct research will find a rewarding array of options and opportunities.

—BRIAN SOLIS, FOUNDER AND PRINCIPAL, FUTUREWORKS

GOALS FIRST: WHAT DOES SUCCESS LOOK LIKE?

Setting goals is a step that many libraries choose to skip over, believing that their mere presence on a social network is the only goal. Do not, repeat, *do not* allow your library to enter social media without knowing what it wants to get out of it! If there is no clear picture of what "success" means, your library isn't ready to enter these communities. It's essential to figure out what your library wants from its efforts and how it plans to achieve a successful outcome.

What might goals for a library social media program look like? After all, when there isn't a specific product to sell, how can you measure success? It doesn't have to be very complicated. Some examples might be the following:

- More people at events and programs
- Better overall awareness of the library
- More blog subscribers
- New knowledge about your patrons and how they view the library
- More "buzz" about the library

Focus on just a few goals, no more than three to begin with. Keep these at the forefront of all of your library's social media work. Whenever your library posts a status update or uploads some kind of media, look at the list of goals and see which one it's contributing to. If the answer is "none," reframe it or drop it and do something that will better serve the library's objectives.

If one of your library's goals is engaging with patrons, then make sure that you're always trying to answer the question, Will this post/update/item cause more patrons to start a conversation with the library? Chances are, if your library is simply promoting a program, it's unlikely to elicit any real response. Efforts to engage patrons may require creativity and planning to be effective.

The next step is to figure out how you're actually going to measure your goals. For instance, will you quantify "buzz" as a certain number of blog comments or Facebook wall posts? Can you quantify "awareness" with a particular number of retweets? If you can't find a way to measure whether or not you're meeting the goal, then the goal is likely not a good one or needs to be refocused. As with any new undertaking, it's important to know how to benchmark results in order to evaluate the undertaking as a whole. Otherwise, you won't know if your efforts are worthwhile in the long run.

BOTTOM LINE

Figuring out your library's social media goals doesn't have to be terribly complex, but it does have to be the first step.

Choosing Social Media Sites

A question I am frequently asked is, What social media should my library spend time on? There are, of course, pros and cons to each, and new networks are appearing all the time. It certainly makes the most sense to invest time in only those that are popular and have critical mass. But how do you know which those are? Libraries are often short of both time and staff and need to be able to focus their efforts where they will really count.

In the case of a business, a social media strategist would begin by investigating which social networks most closely match the target demographic for that business. This can be more difficult to do in the case of a library, which draws patrons from many different demographic profiles. Since the likely goal is to reach as many people as possible with the least amount of effort, it makes sense for a library to pick those sites that are most popular. Beyond popularity, the library needs to be able to support the type of content featured on a particular social site. For instance, if a library isn't planning to release new, original videos regularly, YouTube will not be a good choice.

Keep the library's objectives in mind as well. Assuming that at least one of the library's goals is to converse directly with patrons, make sure that the site supports ways to send messages and share links.

Lastly, conduct some in-house market research. Poll your patrons! You may be surprised to find most are on MySpace rather than on Facebook, or vice versa. It's never ideal to guess at what your patrons want. Instead, begin your library's immersion in social interaction in the offline world; ask people what social media they participate in. This is also a good way to gather a core interest group to which you can promote your new social media presence.

BOTTOM LINE

There is no single "right" social media service that will fit every library. Spend time doing research with patrons and know what kind of content your library can consistently support.

Comparing Social Media Sites

When you start doing your research, it's important to know what kind of social media your library is interested in. A blog is not the same as a social networking site, which is a very broad-based social tool. Social networking sites also are not the same as microblogging sites (e.g., Twitter, where posts are extremely short and functionality is much more limited).

As pointed out previously, social media sites come and go. A good way to find feature comparisons of the most popular sites of the moment is to search online. Side-by-side comparison charts are easy to find via your favorite search engine, but be very sure that you are using the correct terminology in your searches. For example, searching for "social networking sites comparison" may not bring up microblogging tools such as Twitter or Plurk; in other words, be sure you're doing "apples to apples" comparisons.

There are hundreds of sites in this genre, so make sure that your initial research includes obtaining the most recent metrics possible. As of this writing, some major social media websites have hit mainstream use. Some of these may be better suited for your library's needs than others. Table 2.1 gives you some basic demographics for the three social media sites that libraries are the most likely to use.

If your library's decision is going to be based primarily on numbers, there's no question that Facebook is at the top of the heap. Not only does it have the highest

TABLE 2.1 **Basic Demographics for Top Social Media Sites**

	Average age*	Number of users†	Percentage male†	Percentage female†
Facebook	38	400 million	43%	57%
Twitter	39	75 million	42%	58%
MySpace	31	100 million	35%	65%

*As of February 2010   †As of November 2009

number of active users, but more than 50 percent of those users log in to their Facebook accounts every day and more than 1.5 million businesses have pages on the site.[1] No matter the size of your library, if it can choose only one place to have a social media presence, Facebook is almost certainly the best bet across most demographics.

As widespread as Facebook use is, however, it may not be the only place your library should be. Once again, you'll need to go back to your original goals. Not every social media tool will be a good fit for your objectives. For example, if you are using social media primarily to spread the word about an upcoming tax levy, MySpace is probably not a good choice. Not only is the average age of MySpace users younger (meaning that a good part of the demographic is not even old enough to vote), but also your library's content is not a good match for the kinds of content that these users want. On the other hand, if you are looking mostly to have a presence that may create more conversations with teens, MySpace may be the way to go. Figures 2.1–2.3 summarize the kinds of content that users seek on Facebook, MySpace, and Twitter. Note that Twitter is a significantly better tool for spreading breaking news than either Facebook or MySpace. If your library needs to get a message out urgently, Twitter is the best pick by far. This is a reason why libraries should, whenever possible, maintain at least a Twitter *and* a Facebook account. They are different tools with different strengths.

BOTTOM LINE

If your library can be in only one place online, Facebook should be it. Ideally, however, your library should maintain an active presence at least on Facebook and Twitter. They are very different social instruments with different strenghts. Find the best fit for your library based on the demographics you are trying to reach and your library's goals.

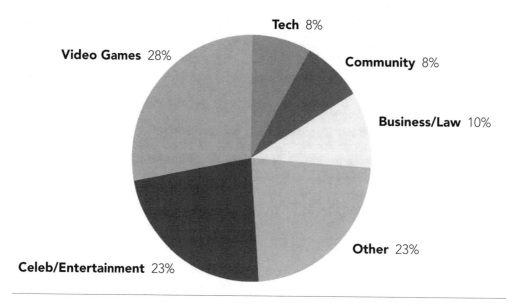

FIGURE 2.1 **MySpace Content Breakdown**

STAFF NEXT: WRITING A SOCIAL MEDIA POLICY FOR STAFF

Many social media experts clearly state that every organization should have a social media policy. The very public nature of social media services does bring some potential hazards that should be addressed. Stories abound of awkward incidents involving social media and oversharing or hotheaded comments. (There's even a website devoted to embarrassing Facebook threads, www.failbooking.com.)

It's unrealistic (and counterproductive) to ban a library's employees from using social media or mentioning their workplace online. A better approach is to plainly spell out some guidelines that employees should keep in mind. A social media policy can go a long way toward preventing PR fiascoes.

Ellyssa Kroski, writing for *School Library Journal*, laid out several criteria that should be included in such a policy.[2] The most important of these are as follows:

- **Include a disclaimer.** Some sort of statement should be included on blogs and social sites where the employee points out that his or her statements are not those of his or her employer, the library.
- **Don't share confidential information.** This includes information about coworkers or patrons or information that is sensitive in nature.
- **Use good judgment.** Employees should always consider the image they might be portraying of the library. Everything an employee posts will be archived by search engines, permanently. Remember the newspaper test: if the post wouldn't survive scrutiny in a newspaper

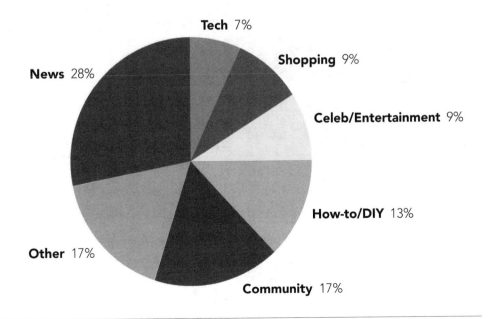

FIGURE 2.2 **Facebook Content Breakdown**

or some other vehicle of mass media distribution, it's not appropriate. If in doubt, they should consult the employee manual or a supervisor.

- **Respect copyright law and accuracy.** Employees should give credit when they quote others, regardless of which social media site they may be using. A direct link to the quoted material is the preferable convention. If something later turns out to be inaccurate, the employee needs to take full responsibility and post a retraction or correction. It's far better to admit a mistake quickly than to attempt to camouflage or ignore it.

A social media policy doesn't have to be a long, wordy document. The point is not to cover every possible contingency or make using social media so intimidating for the library's employees that they won't want to engage in it. Rather, the idea is to show that the library actually supports employees' efforts and acknowledges social media as something that staff very likely want to participate in. Providing written guidelines gives these employees a strong foundation on which to stand.

Some excellent examples of library social media policies include the following:

- University of Texas Southwestern Medical Center Library (http://units .sla.org/chapter/ctx/UTSouthwesternLibrarySocialMediaPolicy_LLT_ Final.pdf)
- Whitman Public Library (www.wmrls.org/policies/6regions/pdf/ whitman.pdf)

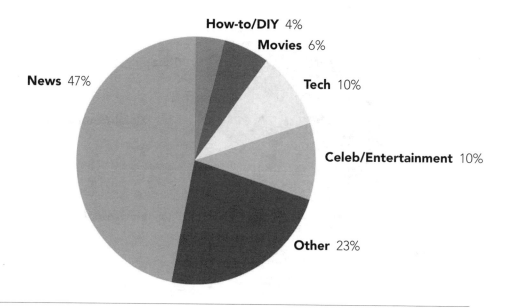

FIGURE 2.3 **Twitter Content Breakdown**

If you'd like to examine social media policies from other nonprofits, government agencies, and various kinds of businesses, try the Social Media Governance Policy Database (http://socialmediagovernance.com/policies.php), which is fully searchable and has more than 120 examples.

BOTTOM LINE
Effective social media involvement takes time and planning.
Don't skip these steps.

NOTES

1. Facebook Facts & Figures (history & statistics), 2010, www.website-monitoring.com/blog/2010/03/17/facebook-facts-and-figures-history-statistics/.

2. Ellyssa Krosky, "Should Your Library Have a Social Media Policy?" 2009, www.schoollibraryjournal.com/article/CA6699104.html.

3

UNDERSTANDING SOCIAL CAPITAL

Those who ignore the party/conversation/network when they are content and decide to drop in when they need the network may not succeed. It's pretty easy to spot those that are just joining the network purely to take—not to give. Therefore, be part of the party/conversation/network before you need anything from anyone.

—JEREMIAH OWYANG, WEB-STRATEGIST.COM

During the Save Ohio Libraries movement in 2009, some libraries in Ohio jumped into Twitter. Undoubtedly, they saw Twitter as another avenue for getting the word out about the imminent and catastrophic budget cuts being proposed by Ohio's governor. However, there were two major factors preventing them from really using Twitter as an effective avenue for rallying support:

1. **Lack of followers**. Numbers are not the only criterion for social media success (and certainly not the most important one), but *some* followers are needed to spread a message. When an organization jumps into a social media tool during a crisis, rather than before, there is a distinct lack of audience to hear any pleas for help.

2. **Lack of social capital.** Social capital is what allows any organization or individual to make requests of its followers successfully. Think of social capital like funds in a sort of intangible bank account; you add to the account by listening to, engaging with, and doing favors for others. Each time you make a request, you are drawing on that account. If no social capital has been established from which to draw, actions requested of others are likely to be ignored.

Having social capital is, in many ways, equivalent to having credibility in a selected online community. It means that others recognize you as someone who provides value and promotes content from others in addition to your own. Social capital can only be earned over time by participating appropriately in the community.

EARNING SOCIAL CAPITAL

Gaining social capital really means becoming a strong, consistent member of the online community. People expect reciprocity; it is important to remember that a good reputation offline does not necessarily translate into social capital online. Although your library may gain followers or friends based on reputation alone, they may or may not engage with or advocate for your library. Building a social media reputation means giving back.

How can your library go about earning the trust of its patrons online? There are several ways, and like all relationships, these methods require effort and time to develop. For most, a combination of the following actions will usually benefit a library's online reputation.

Thank People

People like to be recognized for their contributions. When someone comments on your library blog, even if it's just to agree, thank him or her. If the commenter says something negative, express appreciation for the feedback. It shows that your library is listening to all points of view and values constructive input. If someone posts something about the library to their Facebook page or retweets for your library on Twitter, acknowledge and thank that person. It's an easy way to engage your patrons and can promote positive feelings toward the library.

Ask for Opinions

Nearly everyone likes to be asked for an opinion. Ask for readers' favorite Oprah book pick or their favorite program at the library. Try asking for opinions on the worst book ever written! The more controversial the question, the more feedback it likely will get. Although generating controversy for its own sake may not be your library's goal, facilitating conversation between the library and others is. Don't wait for someone else to start a discussion; be proactive and initiate exchanges of ideas and opinions.

Link to Others

It's very common to pass along interesting links via social media channels. However, posting only links to your library's assets (e.g., catalog, programs, or website) is just another method of self-promotion and not a form of engagement. Have you seen a funny video on YouTube? Pass the link along. Do the same for interesting blog posts and articles. Just make sure they are not written by anyone from your library or you may diminish the open forum you are trying to encourage.

Retweet Others

If your library is on Twitter, the person who is responsible for the Twitter account should learn the syntax of retweeting and do so whenever and as often as possible. Typically, a retweet starts with "RT @[Twitter handle of person being retweeted]." For example: "RT @laurasolomon I'm so glad my library allows me to reserve books online!" You can also add a brief commentary, such as "Yes we do! RT @laurasolomon I'm so glad my library allows me to reserve books online." If one of your library's followers says something that might be of interest to others, pass it along. Bear in mind that you may ask your followers to pass on something later to advocate for the library. Build up your social capital now, so that you can ask for favors later.

Give Credit

This applies to all content, not just retweets. Do you want to promote a new program that was a patron's idea? Name the patron and link directly to that person if you can. An old newspaper adage is that "names sell papers." The library may not be selling anything in the literal sense, but the concept holds. People want to be involved when they know their name is going to be promoted. This is another reason why photos of patrons at programs are a popular way to get people to visit a website; people invariably want to see themselves or someone they know. The library is an organization that cannot exist without its community, so be sure to acknowledge that community whenever possible.

Encourage Others

One way that many people commonly use social media is as an outlet for venting their frustrations. This is the perfect opportunity for your library to hone its social media "voice." Frustrated people often just want to be heard. If one of your library's friends or followers is venting, expressing sympathy can help forge a relationship. It can also serve to show that your library is "human"—that real people who care work there. It also shows that the library is paying attention to its patrons, and its response can help them feel important.

Ask and Tell

People like to have opportunities to talk about themselves. Ask people in your library's network about items they post or follow up on something they posted earlier. In addition to asking, tell them about interesting things that happen at the library. This isn't promoting a program—this is a more personal, less self-serving kind of status update. Maybe you received a unique or interesting reference question? Post it along with the answer. Pique people's interest in what you do and what makes the library "tick."

Provide Something People Care About

Online, your library needs to provide value to its friends and followers. If there's information about something happening in your community, use online channels to pass on that information. When promoting a library event, be sure your post answers this question for your followers: What's in it for me? Advertising a service or program without promoting its benefits is counterproductive and can actually hurt your library's social capital. It's very likely that your patrons are generally overwhelmed with input from various sources throughout their day and are suffering from information fatigue. Most have learned to be picky and are likely to tune out things they find irrelevant or equivalent to pure advertising.

Monitor What People Are Saying and Respond

Social media serves especially well as a listening post to find out what people are saying about your library. When someone says something about your library, whether positive or negative, it's crucial to respond with *something*. Acknowledging the other person and demonstrating that your library is listening (and cares) is extremely important in building one-to-one relationships.

BOTTOM LINE

Every time your library directly engages with someone online in a positive way, especially one that benefits the other person, it gains social capital. Social capital takes time to earn and trust to build.

ADVANCED SOCIAL CAPITAL STRATEGIES

Once your library has been around the social media block a few times, it may be ready to move on to some bolder methods for gaining capital and strengthening relationships. Your library may want to try some of these strategies.

Pictures

Get an account on a Twitter-enabled service, such as Twitpic or Yfrog, that allows you to post photos from anywhere and share them through your library's Twitter account. Think about putting up not only photos of events or programs but also casual or funny shots of staff going about their daily work (or perhaps celebrating a staff birthday). Pictures can also add to the "humanness" of the library online and can add variety to what would normally be only a stream of text posts.

Customer Service

Social media, as a medium, is not always ideal for regular reference service. However, chances are good that your library will occasionally encounter requests for help via social media. Some people prefer to communicate via Facebook message or via tweet. Respect that these people want to communicate with the library and respond, as best as possible, using the same medium.

Contests

If your library runs contests, announce the winners via social media in addition to any other avenues you might use. Try a contest done entirely via social media, such as creating online videos or captioning a photo on Flickr.

Business Cards and Signage

Nowadays, most libraries have their website URL included on their business cards, stationary, ads, and signs. Include your social media URLs in offline promotional materials as well. This acts as social proof, welcoming patrons to your community and building trust in your library. Integrating online and offline advertising not only is common sense but also increases your library's credibility in the social online realms.

Create a Viral Experience

One of the best examples of viral marketing is described by the Twittown blog:

> When the San Francisco area's most famous (er, only) Korean BBQ Take-Out Truck rolls into the neighborhood, lines literally stretch around the block. But given the mobile nature of the business, how do people know when and where to find it? Enter Twitter. Kogi BBQ uses Twitter to let their customers know where they are going to be each day, and if the photographs showing hundreds of people waiting in line for Korean BBQ To-Go are any indicator, it's a business strategy that has worked out incredibly well for them. The real-time nature of their business demands a real-time communications platform to underpin it, and Twitter (as well as Facebook) is the basis for that platform. Sandwich carts around the country should take note.[1]

How many libraries have bookmobiles? This is a strategy that could easily be duplicated. Using social media or texting, the library could create real-time updates and commentary along the bookmobile's route.

Social media participants have to be aware of their deposits and withdrawals of social capital. Having a healthy balance is integral to being successful in the long term. Deposits of social capital add value to the community as a whole; withdrawals only have value to the library.

BOTTOM LINE

Participate in conversations. Remember that the recipients of any of your library's messages have expectations of reciprocity.

SPENDING SOCIAL CAPITAL

Ben McConnell, a writer for the Church of the Customer blog (www.churchofcustomer .com) recommends a social capital deposit/withdrawal ratio of 80 to 20 percent; the vast majority of an individual's or organization's social media interactions need to be other-centered.[2]

Knowing that social capital should be spent only when necessary, you should ration it for only critical purposes. Promoting every program going on at your library will quickly run your social media account into overdraft status. Self-promotion is expensive. The Save Ohio Libraries campaign drew heavily on the social capital of a handful of individuals who were already well invested in social media communities. Advocacy is certainly one legitimate use for social capital. Some other worthwhile purposes include the following:

- Breaking news ("Sorry, the Internet is down—we're working on it!")
- Feedback ("What do you think of the new self-checkout machines?")
- Informal polls ("Which is better: storytimes on weekends or weeknights? Why?")

Yes, do promote the library's programs, but advertise just those that are high-profile or that you know are a great match for your social media audience.

BOTTOM LINE

*Every time your library promotes something or asks for a favor,
it is making a withdrawal. If your withdrawals exceed deposits,
your library effectively becomes a community leech . . .
and in some cases, a pariah. Spend social capital wisely.*

NOTES

1. "Five Wickedly Clever Ways to Use Twitter," 2009, http://twittown.com/social-networks/ social-networks-blog/five-wickedly-clever-ways-use-twitter/.
2. Ben McConnell, "The Last Temptation of Twitter," 2009, www.churchofcustomer .com/2008/12/an-8020-rule-for-selfpromotion.html.

4

STRATEGIES FOR SOCIAL MEDIA SUCCESS

Social media is a long sell process. You are developing content in order to gain an order of trust with people in your area of influence. We are now experiencing a relationship driven economy . . . get on the train.

—KYLE LACY, AUTHOR OF *TWITTER MARKETING FOR DUMMIES*

Warren Sukernek, a social media strategist, tells the story of how he made a reservation at a hotel for a family vacation to Disneyland. He later discovered that the hotel had a Twitter account and even offered a better rate for Twitter users. Sukernek quickly changed his reservation and got the better rate. He sent a tweet to the hotel to inform them of his arrival and thanking them for the great discount. To his surprise, he got no response. Once at the hotel, he received excellent service and had very nice accommodations. He even tweeted this. Still no response.

What Sukernek's story demonstrates is a common failure in social media: the misconception that it's merely a way to broadcast messages or promotions. Despite his overall favorable experience at the hotel, Sukernek no doubt felt let down that the hotel didn't want (or care) to actually converse with him via Twitter. Considering that the hotel actually had a Twitter account and Sukernek was advocating for its brand via that medium, it's surprising that the hotel did not have a follow-up plan for engaging with customers. Whether by benign neglect or deliberate omission, when communication is only one way, it demonstrates that the party initiating the message doesn't want or really care about a response. Perhaps that wasn't the intent of the hotel in Sukernek's anecdote, but the effect was the same: the hotel lost a prime opportunity to build a one-to-one relationship with one of its new customers simply by its apparent ignorance of customer expectations in social media.

There are a good number of social media best practices, some of which I discuss below. Become familiar with them and implement them.

SOCIAL MEDIA PROFILES

One common element of all social media sites is the ability for participants to include some personal information about themselves. The amount and type may vary but nearly all allow for at least a name, a location, a website URL, and an avatar (image). Some have additional fields, such as a short bio, interests, and contact information. Regardless of what options are available, make sure that your library fills out all the information it possibly can. Potential friends and followers will look at profiles in order to determine whether they want your library in their network.

Always remember *why* your library is in this space—to connect with others. How many people will want to connect with something that they cannot identify as authentic or relevant?

Your library's profile is, in many cases, the main opportunity it will have in a particular network to establish trust. The burden of credibility is on you, so being as complete as possible is key. All too often libraries fail to include simple things such as their logo. (Don't use a photo of your building; library buildings are almost never the same as a brand, and many avatars will be displayed at too small a size to display any real identifying details.)

Once you have your library's profiles set up, move on to the following "next steps."

Get a Vanity URL

On Facebook, once your library's page has twenty-five or more fans, you can convert the long, unwieldy default URL into something easy to remember, such as www.facebook .com/examplelibrary. This makes it infinitely easier for interested patrons to find your library. Add this URL to your library's print promotional materials and business cards. Also add a direct link using the Facebook logo on your library's blogs and websites.

Link Your Profiles

Many social media sites allow you to connect your accounts. For example, you can synchronize your Twitter updates to your Facebook posts, so you only have to post in one place and it shows up in two. LinkedIn has various applications to import your status updates from other sites as well. This strategy not only simplifies your library's social media work, but it also can help cross-promote the library's various social media presences.

Install Applications

Some sites, such as Facebook and LinkedIn, allow you to customize a profile with various types of add-ons (applications, or "apps"). Some are useful, and some are just for fun.

You will likely find some apps that are useful for making your profile more interesting or more interactive. Even some of the fun apps, such as "Pieces of Flair" on Facebook, can help you promote your library's brand in a whimsical way. This app allows you to create a virtual button (like a campaign button) with your library's logo (or any image) on it that you can then send to your friends. This might be a creative and entertaining way to engage your friends and promote your library's brand.

Customize

Sites such as Twitter and MySpace allow users to create custom backgrounds for their profile pages. Be sure to take full advantage of this feature by using your library's logo clearly in the background image.

BOTTOM LINE

As library staff, we know that people do judge books by their covers. Your library's social media profiles are "covers" that people will use to judge the library. Put effort into making them interesting, authentic, and inviting.

LEARNING THE COMMUNITY

When attending an event, it is the rare individual who can simply rush in and start chatting with the first person he or she encounters. Most people are likely to survey the crowd for a bit first in order to get a feel for any group dynamics that might be in play. This instinct is a particularly good one when it comes to social media. Once your library has set up its account on a given service, take some time to get the "lay of the land." Even if you have some experience with other social media networks, you may be surprised to learn that the customs of one are not necessarily the same as another. For example, what your library does on Twitter will likely be significantly different from what it does on Facebook. Twitter is excellent for sharing breaking news, while Facebook is significantly better for longer posts and for publicizing upcoming events and anecdotes that may interest others.

One way to illustrate this is to do a comparison of popular social media sites Facebook and Twitter. Many people use both, because each serves a different purpose and has different customs. Looking at Table 4.1, it might be simple to guess where it would be best to promote a program that is happening in the next several weeks, as compared with announcing an Internet service outage. There is certainly overlap in users between the two services, but people will tailor their posts to the medium. A researcher at Microsoft Research New England, danah boyd (she legally changed her name to all lowercase), ponders the differences on her blog:

> Different social media spaces have different norms. You may not be able to describe them, but you sure can feel them. Finding the space that clicks with

you is often tricky, just as finding a voice in a new setting can be. This is not to say that one space is better than the other. I don't believe that at all. But I do believe that Facebook and Twitter are actually quite culturally distinct and that trying to create features to bridge them won't actually resolve the cultural differences.[1]

As tempting as it might be to jump right in, it may be better to first observe the conversational syntaxes happening around you. This may well save your library from committing an egregious faux pas.

BOTTOM LINE

*If your library chooses to participate in more than one social network,
be sure it understands the different cultures and uses of each.
Social media communities have different expectations of communication.*

BEING TRANSPARENT

At its core, building relationships is all about building trust. Trust can only come when both parties are open about what they are doing and what they are feeling. This means participating in social media truly necessitates being transparent. People who connect with your library often will want to know more about what's going on behind the

TABLE 4.1 **Comparison of Facebook and Twitter**

Facebook	Twitter
■ Best for connecting with people you already know	■ Best for connecting with people you don't know
■ Better for posts that are not time sensitive	■ Better for time-sensitive posts
■ Better for local news/events	■ Better for content that is not localized
■ Conversations happen less in real time	■ Conversations happen more in real time
■ Can post updates that are fairly wordy	■ Limited to 140-character updates
■ More emphasis on deep connections	■ More emphasis on follower counts
■ Complex functionality; somewhat more difficult to use	■ Simple functionality; easier to use
■ Has replaced e-mail and IM for many	■ Has replaced RSS for many

scenes—they're looking for a more personal experience. The more you can give them that experience, the deeper the sense of connection there may be.

Continuous, open communications are an important part of developing a relationship. But how can a library do this? Here are a few suggestions.

Find Your Library's Voice

Remember that people are viewing your library as yet another node in their social network. This means it's essentially the equivalent of any other person in that network. So talk like a person! Be human. Ditch the institutional jargon. Get rid of the formal tone. Social media is much more casual than most other forms of communication. Ideally, your library will have one person doing its social media work, so that the library's voice will be consistent. However, if more than one person contributes, be sure that all of the participants understand the kind of language that will constitute online communications.

Talk about the Challenges of Your Library

It's often easier to put on a good face and only give people the upbeat or happy news. But we live in a world filled with difficult news as well. Show both sides of your library's "personality" by sharing issues that may be troubling. Let people know the library is worried that the upcoming levy may not pass. Tell them you're just as annoyed by the self-check machines being down as they are. Show that there are human beings behind the profile who have feelings and frustrations. Be careful, though, not to let this avenue turn into a steady stream of complaints.

Explain Changes

Did your library have to stop buying some materials due to budget cuts? Were new self-check machines installed? Whatever the decision, use social media not only to inform but also to explain and clarify. One business owner I know will spend hours explaining the reasoning behind even minor decisions to his employees. Over time, he has found that it helps them to empathize with the store's position if customers complain and helps them feel more a part of the business. Take the time to give as much information as is reasonably possible and let your patrons feel that they are a part of the library.

Own Up to Your Mistakes

One of the most important parts of being transparent is being honest. If you give out incorrect information, make a public correction and apologize clearly for the error. If your library does something that garners negative feedback, don't try to hide from it.

Address it directly and publicly. Organizations make mistakes, just as people do. Stand out from the crowd by coming clean about them.

Talk about Individual Staff

"Did you know that Susan, the storytime lady, is a competitive salsa dancer? We didn't know either until last week!" Or, "Thank goodness for Jim, who knows how to do a mail merge in OpenOffice." (Of course, be sure that you have permission from the staff members you want to post about.) Let people see behind the scenes and connect to individuals in your library.

BOTTOM LINE

Be human and talk like a human in your social media interactions. Be authentic and honest, and connections and conversations will follow.

UNDERSTAND THE PEOPLE WHO CONNECT

Just like any other form of patron interaction, understanding the audience is crucial. Regardless of what social media network your library chooses, some characteristics of its users will remain generally the same. Keeping these things in mind will help your library be more effective in the social media space.

People Are Busy—REALLY Busy

This is part of the appeal of social media: people can stay connected to those they know without having to sacrifice large blocks of time. Be sure whatever you post is worth the time of the people who will read it. This comes back to the idea of adding value when you participate in social media.

In addition, be aware that constant status updates can be interpreted as spam behavior. I have seen libraries put out a stream of five or more consecutive tweets in the morning, all promoting programs, and then nothing—no interaction and nothing later in the day. Not only was there no value to these tweets for the average follower, but there also were so many so close together that I began to tune them out. With some of these libraries, I felt forced to "unfollow" them, as they simply filled up my Twitter stream with useless messages.

Time is a valuable commodity these days for everyone. Just because a library is a not-for-profit organization with loyal patrons is no excuse for overwhelming fans and followers. Show people you value their time, and they will be more likely to value your library in return.

People Want to Look Good

When people can share something unique and interesting with their network of friends, it helps them to accumulate social capital. Every time that your library's posts can help someone look like they are smart, have special status, or are "in the know," it's a win-win situation. The person sharing what you shared looks good to friends, and your library, as the enabler, gets social capital as the result of having done a favor. In addition, the library has helped start a conversation.

If the library reposts something someone else on the network has said (e.g., retweeting), that makes people look good, too. It is a direct affirmation of the worth of the content's originator.

BOTTOM LINE

No matter what social network your library chooses to participate in, always remember that people appreciate the value of content. Don't waste people's time with posts or status updates that are just worthless fillers.

RESPONSE TIME MATTERS

In April of 2009, Amazon.com apologized to Twitter users after the sales rankings and some search results for gay and lesbian literature quietly disappeared from the merchant's site. The apology came after a tremendous online uproar with much negative criticism of Amazon and unfriendly commentary about Amazon's new label of "adult" for the genre. The social media backlash was obviously unexpected by the online retailer. What was more surprising, however, was the further and extensive criticism leveled at Amazon for its slow response time to the hue and cry of its customers. When Amazon failed to respond to commentary within a day, the social media world emphatically labeled the company as uncommunicative.

Companies and organizations are learning, much to their chagrin, that communication is now 24/7. It used to be, with traditional offline media, that if a crisis happened on a Friday, you likely had the weekend to think about a response and then could implement that response the following Monday. In the social media world, twenty-four hours is a *very* long time. Amazon.com could have avoided at least some of the backlash simply by communicating more quickly; it failed to consider that the accelerated time frame within which social media operates can turn a relatively routine incident into a marketing crisis.

Social media happens in real or almost-real time. Participating in conversations as they happen is an absolute must for the successful organization today. Preventing a marketing crisis is not the only reason to monitor social media constantly, however. For a library, timeliness is more likely to come into play when responding to simple questions or comments. Don't let even positive posts wait! Just as your fans and followers want your content, they also want your attention. When they don't get it in what they perceive to be a timely manner, chances are good they'll feel rejected and may even cease connecting (e.g., "defriending," "unfollowing").

BOTTOM LINE

Social media, in many cases, is happening in close to real time.
Failure to respond promptly to a conversation, either positive or negative,
can result in a great deal of harm to your library's reputation.

PICKING LIBRARY FRIENDS

In earlier days of social media, it was not uncommon to see libraries with social media accounts where the library had only allowed other libraries, librarians, or perhaps authors to be "friends" of the account. Often, this was a misguided attempt to somehow gain control in a medium that is inherently very open. Sometimes, it was a lack of understanding on the part of a library's board or administrators about what social media really is.

Unfortunately, misperceptions still persist. Recently, I was contacted by a frustrated librarian whose library had a MySpace account. The librarian "friended" anyone who wanted to be MySpace friends, believing that the library should be accessible to all. It later turned out that some of the friends had some questionable content on their profiles. The administration reacted by severely criticizing the librarian and shutting down the entire account.

This particular reaction raises several issues:

- Part of the administration's overreaction was likely due to a misconception about how to approach social media. Traditional marketing and reputation management resolutions are not applicable. Libraries need to understand that successful social media has a human tone. Being human means having human friends, not necessarily paragons of what we may expect our patrons to be.
- Another likely reason for this response may have resulted from a misunderstanding of what the term *friend* means in social media. The word does not have the same connotations as it does offline, and rarely does it refer to an actual close, personal bond.
- Whatever is on a person's profile reflects on that person and not necessarily on the connecting friends. Unless the profile is somehow directly harming the library's reputation, I just don't see the argument that the library is somehow responsible for this content. After all, we

TABLE 4.2 **"Friending" Policy Guidelines**

Keep	Ignore/Block
■ Business or organization in your library's service area	■ Business or organization that is not in your library's service area and/or has nothing to do with libraries
■ People, even if they are not in your service area	■ People, regardless of location, who use highly sexualized avatars (these are almost always spambots, not real people)
■ People who mention the library online	■ People or organizations that are overly self-promotional and/or constantly trying to sell something

are not personally responsible for every silly picture or off-the-wall comment that our friends post online.

■ Why is the library screening patrons at its virtual door that it would allow to enter its physical one? Why is the library's presence online only open to some and not to all?

Stories like this one serve to emphasize there is a great deal of confusion in libraries about how to handle actual connections (friends, followers, fans, etc.) in social media. Who *should* a library connect to? Who should it avoid? Should it be a completely open online forum? There are no truly hard and fast rules to follow in this regard. Table 4.2 shows some important criteria libraries can use to guide them in forming their own "friending" policies.

What about the idea of only connecting to other libraries or librarians? As mentioned previously, this is an outdated approach. There are three main problems with this: (1) it discriminates against anyone who's not in a "library" category; (2) it will be immediately apparent when potential friends/followers look at your library's profile that they are not likely welcome (What patron will want to connect with something that only connects to entities that typically have logos?); and (3) perhaps most significant, it totally ignores the whole precept of social media—to connect to a community at large.

Another common problem I've encountered (especially on Twitter) is the library that follows *no one* back. These are likely libraries that believe social media is just another way to broadcast their message and indicates a tremendous failure to understand the potential of the medium. Not making any connections also indicates the library has no interest in listening to its patrons—not a message any institution would want to send, even inadvertently. Make sure your follower ratio is somewhat even; your library should be following back roughly the same number of people following it.

DON'T ABANDON YOUR FANS

Social media takes time, work, and a sense of commitment. It's something that must be tended to daily, much like brushing your teeth. Once your library starts acquiring friends and followers, there is an unspoken obligation to communicate regularly with them. People friend/follow with the assumption that your library will be imparting content of some interest to them.

Eventually, some of these followers will fall off to pursue other interests. However, if your library fails to post regularly, it will lose followers much more quickly, in much the same way that an apparently abandoned blog will lose readership. Use both status updates and varied conversations with followers to maintain a constant stream of communication.

EMPOWERING LIBRARY STAFF

This is something that can be especially difficult for library administrators to grasp. They are not alone; many for-profit workplaces restrict access to social media by employees, mistakenly believing this will somehow allow the company to control what employees do and say during work hours. Inevitably, these employees find ways around such restrictions and may end up saying more negative things about their place of employment than they might have otherwise.

Smart organizations have come to realize empowered employees make for powerful and effective social media channels. Zappos.com is often cited as a company that gets social media right; it not only uses Twitter effectively to build its customer base but also actively encourages its employees to tweet. Tony Hsieh, the CEO of Zappos.com, says this of his company's Twitter policy:

> I think it's important for employees to be able to express their individuality. We want our customers to feel like they are interacting with real people, not a faceless corporation.[2]

Undoubtedly, this will make some people leery. Won't staff waste inordinate amounts of time on social media? Kyle Lacy, the author of *Twitter Marketing for Dummies*, says:

> It is time to stop being afraid of the massive force of online communication. It is time to stop putting firewalls up because you're afraid your employees are not being productive. They are not being productive for a reason . . . and it's not Facebook. If they love what they do . . . maybe it is time to allow them to communicate that fact . . . and if they don't . . . you probably have more problems than communication.[3]

If your library would like to follow in the footsteps of Tony Hsieh, you can encourage staff to share specific types of content. Some of these might include:

- **Events.** Suggest that staff help promote major (not minor) events. Employees should also indicate if they are attending.
- **Awards.** If your library receives a community award or is ranked highly by such surveys as Hennepin or *Library Journal* 5-Star Libraries, ask employees to help spread the word. They can help make your local community proud of its library.
- **Extraordinary promotions.** If your library does something like "Food for Fines," staff could help get the news out. Think of this kind of post as something done maybe three or four times a year, or the novelty will wear off quickly.
- **New blog post.** This isn't to suggest that you ask your staff to promote every new post on the library blog. Rather, ask them to point to blog posts that might be very unusual (e.g., penned by the director) or to those written by third-party individuals that might mention some aspect of the library.
- **New services.** If your library starts doing something both brand-new and on a large scale (e.g., switching to self-check machines), this is a prime opportunity for staff to talk about it and reassure their followers about any concerns.
- **Videos.** Videos can have very powerful click-through rates (especially if they're funny). If your library makes videos for either instruction or entertainment, staff could assist in getting them seen.

BOTTOM LINE

Your library's employees can be a powerful set of connections. Use them to make your library more human, but use them sparingly.

WHO'S IN CHARGE?

There is much debate about exactly who should control an organization's social media presence. Even in the corporate world, there is not a clearly defined answer. In many cases, companies have decided that their public relations staff should manage social media: not only does their title include the word *public*, but they likely possess expertise in speaking to the public without jargon and in clear, concise language. However, this argument doesn't necessarily work for libraries, where the majority of the staff probably works with the public on a daily basis. In fact, one of the most common complaints I hear from librarians is that their library's social media is controlled by the PR department—and the kinds of communication that appear in the library's social media are self-serving, stiff, or even arrogant.

Who's right? And what about the teen librarian? How about the IT department? Some even consider their human resources staff for the job. Obviously, there is not a cut-and-dried answer to this question.

Mary Deming Barber, communications consultant at the Barber Group, says: "Social media is about engagement and conversation, neither of which are strengths of IT or HR. Beyond that, the decision to place 'control' in PR, marketing, communications or other seems to be based on an individual company and its structure."[4]

Barber nails the main issue: social media is about engagement and conversation. The person responsible for the library's social media needs to excel at this. This will not automatically mean the PR person, teen librarian, or any particular position in the library. It's not about title or position. Your library may have a reference librarian handling social media for several months, only to have that person leave. Rather than automatically giving it to the reference librarian's replacement, the successful library will evaluate the staff as a whole to see who is best suited for the job. Does this mean that the maintenance guy could be doing the tweeting? Possibly! The answer to the question of who's in charge of a library's social media is truly situational.

BOTTOM LINE

Don't assign social media work to someone based on title or based on how some other library has delegated the job. Make sure the person you choose is the right fit for the job.

STATUS UPDATE MAKEOVERS

Up until now, we've discussed many ways that libraries can make their use of social media more effective. However, we haven't really looked at concrete examples of both good and bad uses of social media. In this section, we'll look at some examples of social status updates and why they are problematic. I'll also show some ways that these same updates can be remade to be more appealing and more effective.

EXAMPLE ONE

The internet computers are not available due to maintenance.

Why Is This Ineffective?

This update sounds like it came from a robot. It's highly impersonal and is likely to be ignored, turn people off, or both. "Maintenance" is not descriptive and doesn't really say what's going on. In this example, it constitutes generic language.

How Could It Be Better?

People want to know there is a human being behind the account. The only way to do that is to use language that demonstrates a real person is making the post. Remember, part of the reason people will connect to your library is to get more behind-the-scenes information. Give some detail. Transparency is important.

REMADE EXAMPLE ONE

Argh! Power surge took down a server— no Internet here this morning, sorry!

Why Is This Better?

It's easy to tell with the addition of expressive language (i.e., "Argh!") that a real person, with real emotions, is making the post. Additional information is provided that really explains why there is no Internet access at the library today. The simple addition of the word *sorry* at the end of the post shows that the library is sympathetic to those who may have wanted to come in to use the Internet.

EXAMPLE TWO

Helped a patron find a turnip cookbook today.

Why Is This Ineffective?

Whenever the library makes a status update, it has to consider how it will be received. One question to continually ask is, What's in this post for someone else? Another question to ask would be, Why should someone else care? The cookbook in question may have been unique or fascinating, but there's no sense of that in the post. For all the end user knows, requests for turnip cookbooks could be par for the course in a library. There's nothing to indicate this is an unusual request.

How Could It Be Better?

More detail is required to really make this post stand out and possibly spark a conversation. Including a few extra words to help put the comment into context will help.

REMADE EXAMPLE TWO

Helped patron find turnip cookbook. Didn't know there was such a thing!

Why Is This Better?

The main thing that makes this different from the original is the addition of the second sentence. It lets the reader know the cookbook was unique enough to pique the interest of the librarian. It also shows a sense of transparency and openness; the librarian is showing he or she doesn't know everything. Lastly, it adds a very human touch to an otherwise unremarkable post.

EXAMPLE THREE

Cool sailboat craft program at 10 am today!

Why Is This Ineffective?

This status update is fairly typical of most libraries currently using Twitter purely as a broadcast mechanism. The update does nothing beyond promote a program. It gives no reason why anyone would want to attend other than because the library has declared it to be "cool." There is no clue as to the payoff for the reader.

How Could It Be Better?

The subject matter of the craft session (i.e., sailboats) isn't really what the reader will get out of the program. In fact, the reader in this case is not the potential participant but rather the parent. Gear the message accordingly. What will parents get out of it? Why should they bring their kids?

REMADE EXAMPLE THREE

It's noisy, messy, and chaotic, & your kids will love it! Crafts @ 10 am today.

Why Is This Better?

The payoff is much more readily apparent; it's a program with qualities that will be fun for kids, and if parents bring their children, the kids will love the program. Note that the subject of the crafts needn't even be included in such a brief announcement; people will be primarily interested in what they will get out of it. There's also a possibility the lack of craft subject may inspire fans or followers to respond with additional questions, initiating further conversation around the topic and potentially garnering interest from others.

EXAMPLE FOUR

New science fiction and fantasy books at your library [LINK]

Why Is This Ineffective?

Much like example 3, this status update is primarily self-promotional. Aside from that, it's pretty blasé as a status update. It lacks any interesting framework to catch the attention of busy followers. Even a hard-core genre fan may overlook this particular announcement.

How Could It Be Better?

Always remember that your library's fans may be extremely busy, so compose status updates to make it worth their while to read them. Connect the announcement in some way to something that gives it more context.

REMADE EXAMPLE FOUR

New Nebula Award winners just announced!
Request copies at [LINK].

Why Is This Better?

This status update serves two functions: it gives breaking news ("Nebula Award winners just announced!") and it informs interested followers that items in a particular genre are available. It provides additional context for the post that is more likely to gain attention. This strategy has been extended by explaining to readers that the link in the posting will take them directly to the new science fiction and fantasy selections where they can browse and request these titles.

EXAMPLE FIVE

Next week at the library: HOMEWORK HELP CENTER [LINK]

Why Is This Ineffective?

This particular status post is, overall, very uninformative. It makes an assumption that the reader will bother to click through the link in order to get any real information about the program. Keep in mind readers will only click a link if you have caught their interest first. Just because a post is from their local library isn't reason enough to assume fans are tempted by anything it has to say. All-caps usage is also troubling. It is a well-known convention on the Web that all-caps indicates shouting; no fan wants to be yelled at.

How Could It Be Better?

Once again, it's important to give the readers something they want. Readers might want a homework help center, but it would be difficult to know for sure without specifics. Also, because the post originates with a library's social media account, there's not likely to be a need to announce the location of the help center.

REMADE EXAMPLE FIVE

Kids getting worried about report cards?
Homework Help Center begins on
Monday @ 4:00 pm [LINK]

Why Is This Better?

The remade version provides additional context that will help a potential reader decide if he or she is interested in the update. The hook is clear (kids + report cards = worry) and implies the nature of the payoff: kids will get help that may result in better grades. Including a specific date and time is also beneficial, as it give more information up front without making the reader do more work to get it.

MAGAZINES AS ROLE MODELS

One of the best examples for how to do status updates well may come from near the checkout at your local grocery store. The next time you visit, take a careful look at some of the headlines that beckon from the covers of many of the magazines displayed in the racks:

- "Walk Off 10 Pounds in 10 Days"
- "What to Wear Now"
- "Get Back Your Shape"
- "15 Tips for a Bigger Tax Refund"
- "Smart Clothes for Tough Times"
- "How to Look 10 Years Younger"
- "Simple Ways to Declutter Every Room"

Why do magazines use these kinds of headlines? In a word: economy. Not only do they have a limited amount of space on the cover, they also know they have a very brief time in which to capture a potential buyer's attention. In order to tempt someone to buy their publication, magazine editors know that headlines need to be short and sweet and the payoff very clear.

Libraries are actually dealing with a very similar situation, where limited amount of space is available for most status updates and the attention span of potential readers is often very short by necessity. Yet, most libraries fail to capture the attention of their audience because they tend to mistake a status update with a call for action. It's vital for successful long-term use of social media to remember that a call to action draws on social capital. Therefore, nearly every time your library specifically asks followers to exert an effort, especially toward a particular goal of the library (by doing, being, having, checking, joining, seeing, hearing, or coming), that is a withdrawal, not a deposit. Most calls to action don't have anything of inherent value to followers. Remember: calls to action represent the need to ask a favor. Your followers primarily want to know what the library can do for them, not the reverse.

BOTTOM LINE

Make status updates human. Always remember what will be first and foremost in the readers' minds: the payoff. What will they get from your post? If you can't easily answer that question, rewrite.

NOTES

1. danah boyd, "Some Thoughts on Twitter vs. Facebook Status Updates," 2009, www.zephoria.org/thoughts/archives/2009/10/25/some_thoughts_o-3.html.
2. Shannon Nelson, "Improving Brand Value through Social Media: Zappos Gets It Right," 2008, www.piercemattiepublicrelations.com/social_networks/.
3. Kyle Lacy, "Empower Your Employees to Win with Social Media," 2010, http://kylelacy.com/empower-your-employees-to-win-with-social-media/.
4. Rick Alcantara, "Who Should 'Control' Social Media within a Company?" 2010, www.socialmediatoday.com/SMC/183509/.

5

WHAT CAN WE COUNT?

It's not as simple as counting subscribers, followers, fans, conversation volume, reach, or traffic. While the size of the corporate social graph is a reflection of our participation behavior, it is not symbolic of brand stature, resonance, loyalty, advocacy, nor is it an indicator of business performance.

—BRIAN SOLIS, AUTHOR OF *ENGAGE*

Evaluation of social media is still a somewhat murky and controversial subject. There is no single, defined standard for measuring engagement. Rather, there are a host of expert opinions, many of which differ. In addition, most of the methodologies are really meant to be used with businesses that can track concrete factors such as sales. There are, however some things that libraries can and should do. Measuring numbers of fans/followers is certainly one, but it isn't the only one. A library can benefit from investigating both quantitative and qualitative progress, which will likely give a better big-picture view than tracking either outcome alone.

If a library has jumped into social media without really understanding why, its haste becomes apparent when it's time to evaluate progress. If there are no stated goals, there will be no way to measure progress toward them. Libraries first have to know *what they want* from social media before they can determine how effective their efforts have been. Evaluation really begins *before* you measure results.

The first step is to decide your library's social media goals and take a baseline measurement. This allows you to do a comparison during evaluation and later on. Typically, a library should be thinking about the possible effects that have nonfinancial but nonetheless desirable impact. These might include the following:

- Website visitors
- Positive press
- YouTube views
- Blog comments
- Retweets (Twitter)
- Visitors to the physical library
- Positive word of mouth
- Number of friends/fans/followers
- Employment applications
- Social media mentions

For instance, if your library decides that one of its goals is to increase the number of comments on its blogs, figure an average number that a post gets currently. (Most, if not all, blog platforms allow you track the number of comments on a given post.) If the objective is to get more social media mentions, use a tool like Google Alerts to figure out how often your library is already mentioned in a given time period. (Google Alerts will e-mail you any time a particular keyword is mentioned online.) Once you have a baseline number, you can accurately evaluate later to see what progress (if any) has been made.

BOTTOM LINE

You won't know how far your library has come with its social media strategy unless you know where it began. Make sure goals are clear and measurable and baseline measurements are known.

QUANTITATIVE MEASUREMENTS

In the profit sector, evaluation of new programs or products is typically done using ROI, or return on investment. ROI is calculated by subtracting your starting value from your final value, and then dividing that total by the starting value. In other words, if you invest $10 and get back $30, the formula will be $(30 - 10)/10$; your ROI is double the amount of your initial investment.

When it comes to social media, the problem with ROI is that it was never designed to measure human interactions. Even a business with a product to sell will find that trying to justify social media with ROI is imprecise at best and useless at worst. When discussing libraries, which generally don't have products to sell, ROI becomes even more problematic. As I'll explain later, however, ROI as a tool can still help a library measure social media success.

Quantitative measurements that can be tracked include the number of fans or followers. In addition, a library will likely want to track how many people connect to the library in a given period of time within a particular social network. The number of posts to a Facebook wall, Twitter mentions, and so on are also worth tracking to determine the amount of activity and engagement.

MEASURING OPINIONS

Knowing the general "feel" (sentiment analysis) of interactions is also important for gauging how your library is doing in social media. Sentiment, or opinion analysis, should come into play whenever social media is evaluated. After all, an increase in Twitter mentions does little good if most of those mentions express negative opinions.

When doing a measurement, baseline or progressive, it's crucial to know if those measurements constitute positive or negative mentions. This means your library should also be measuring negative effects of social media. If the original goal was to increase the number of blog comments, then knowing how many are positive and how many are negative is going to give you a much better idea of what's going on than just the sum of the comments.

Figuring out a qualitative measurement will require you to take a close look at the original social media goals for your library. If you want to track conversation or engagement, you'll need to establish that baseline measurement mentioned previously. To do this, ask such questions as the following:

- Are we currently part of online conversations about the library/community?
- How is the library talked about online, compared to other, similar (or nearby) libraries or community organizations?

Once you know those answers, you can work on answering these kinds of questions:

- Have we built better relationships with our patrons?
- Are we participating in conversations where previously we didn't have a voice?
- Have we moved from monologue to meaningful dialogue with patrons?

There are a growing number of automated tools that claim to track online sentiment. These include such well-known pay services such as OpenAmplify and Radian6. However, there are some major flaws with these, and human communications are more shades of gray than strictly black and white. The results that come from these types of tools may not result in any kind of accurate perspective. These tools also usually fail to account for the inherent level of influence of different people and different online social sites. A Twitter mention by a famous person will not necessarily have more weight than one by a noncelebrity. Human sentiment is very difficult to measure in an automated way. As of the time of this writing, it's probably best for your library to avoid these kinds of services until they become more sophisticated.

When it comes to sentiment analysis, it doesn't really have to be complex. What you're really looking for are trends or correlations. Does your library see an uptick in program attendance after a positive social media mention? Or is there a decline after a negative one? Or any effect at all? Is there an increase in Facebook wall comments after you post a link to your library's new DVD list, and are they complaints or compliments? This is the kind of analysis that is going to make a difference.

In the end, no matter how adept you might be at online conversation and engagement, it's going to come down to how it ultimately affects your library. The library's administration will need to justify the time and effort spent on this medium, just as it has to do with any other endeavor.

BOTTOM LINE

Numbers aren't enough; it's important to know what those numbers really mean. Monitor the conversations happening in your library's networks and know what the primary nature of those conversations is: negative or positive.

IS BIGGER BETTER?

Nowadays, we often see challenges from one celebrity to another to see who can accumulate the most fans/followers. Perhaps one of the earliest and most well-known of these contests was that of Ashton Kutcher and the CNN network. In early 2009, Kutcher challenged CNN to a race to acquire one million followers on Twitter. Of this competition, Kutcher said: "I found it astonishing that one person can actually have as big of a voice online as what an entire media company can on Twitter."[1] Kutcher ended up not only winning the contest, but he also became the first Twitter user with a million followers.

It's not unusual to see individuals, companies, and organizations attempt to collect friends and followers just for the fun of it or to increase market share or buzz. But in the case of a library, does the size of its online social network mean it has more influence or a bigger potential market for its "product"?

The answer to that question depends on how you define "large." Maureen Evans, a graduate student and poet, found her definition through personal experience. She joined Twitter in its early days in 2006. She soon had 100 followers and enjoyed conversing with them regularly. In 2007, Maureen began a new project, tweeting recipes that she had condensed to 140 characters. She soon had more than 3,000 followers. Nevertheless, her network still felt like a small community, with regulars frequently responding to her and each other. It wasn't until her audience grew to over 13,000 that the dynamic began to significantly change. At that point, the conversation stopped. The sense of community disappeared entirely. "It became dead silence," Maureen said of the change.[2] What happened? Maureen didn't have nearly the fan base that Ashton Kutcher had.

Social networking doesn't scale once the network gets too big. Kutcher may have a million followers, but it's highly unlikely that his fans are as engaged as Evans's were early on. It's easier to know everyone and feel comfortable in a small neighborhood than in a large one. Clive Thompson, a writer for *Wired* magazine, says: "Once a group reaches a certain size, each participant starts to feel anonymous again, and the person they're following—who once seemed proximal, like a friend—now seems larger than life and remote."[3]

The community falls apart once it becomes too large. "Too large" will be defined differently by each participating individual, but it can range from several hundred to several thousand. Celebrities like Kutcher are part of a select echelon of social media participants who can maintain extremely large fan bases simply because there isn't likely to be such an expectation of intimacy with followers. In other words, as Thompson points out, there is a value in relative obscurity.

For libraries, this is good news. Typically, a library will be primarily targeting a local audience, meaning that it will automatically have a smaller fan base to pull from. The chances of having hundreds of thousands of followers are unlikely. What libraries will have to aim for, then, is not necessarily a quantity of connections, but quality. A library should really be seeking followers who will share its content, because even a small number of people reposting library content can be effective and can trump a large number of followers who don't. It's all about sharing and networking. Your library following may only have 50 people in it, but if one of those people has several hundred people following them and reposts your content, that content has a greater potential to be seen.

This is one of the reasons many people want their content to go "viral": to spread their content as far as possible. Of course, part of going viral is having content that people want to share. But the other part is having a network willing to share it. Your library may have thousands of followers, but if they don't retweet or repost your content, it's not a whole lot different from having no followers at all.

BOTTOM LINE

Extremely large numbers of social connections don't usually scale into viable online communities. Focus on connecting with people who will share your content, not on acquiring large numbers of fans or followers.

EVALUATION AND REACH

One way to think about the effects of your library's social media efforts is to consider the idea of *reach*. According to Rebecca Atkinson,[4] a freelance web marketer and analyst, reach is made up of three factors:

1. **Conversation/Mentions.** This refers to reach in the sense of where and how often your library is being talked about. Obviously, the more places and more times your library is being discussed, the better.
2. **Sharing.** The reach of your library can also be considered by examining how many times its content is shared. How many people are retweeting or reposting library content?

3. **Social media referrals.** Another piece of this is to take a close look at the analytics for your library website. How many visitors to the website come from a social media site?

Reach comprises all three of these factors. Adding them together will give you a fairly accurate picture as to how many people your library is reaching through social media channels. Having a concrete idea about how many people are interacting with your library's content is a good way to begin to measure success.

Once you know how many people your library is reaching, the next step is to figure out just how much social media is costing your library. It's probable that your library invested more time than money on social media over a given period. This means that to really know your actual ROI, you will need to know the cost of the staff time. So, as an example, let's say that one staff member, who makes $20 an hour, spends three hours per week on social media for her library. This sample library has the following reach statistics for the past week:

- 10 separate conversations where the library was mentioned
- Content from/about the library shared 15 times
- 58 site visits generated by referrals from social media sites

The total number of people reached this past week was 83. The cost of the efforts to reach these people (staff time) was $60. To get the cost per reach, divide the total of number of people reached by the total cost of the effort. In this case, each reach would cost the library $1.38.

All of this begs the question, Is $1.38 per person a good amount for the library to be spending? This can only clearly be answered by knowing how much actual effect the library's reach has had on the library. This is where you will need to revisit once again the library's goals. Is the library benefiting in some way from these efforts? More patron awareness? More blog comments? More attendees at library programs? Whatever the goal, being able to show a tangible return is really what determines whether or not a social media campaign is successful. Comparing this cost to that of a similar outreach activity such print marketing may help put it in perspective as well.

Your library's ROI is something that also needs to be looked at over the long term. Some weeks/months will be better than others, but it is the long-term trends that will be especially meaningful. This is particularly important in social media where it's likely your social graph will expand over time. The more connections you have (up to a point), the more potential there may be to spread your message. Over longer periods, this will likely mean that you will see increases in some reach criteria. Also, some library content will be more viral than others, resulting in some periods where you may see an activity spike in factors such as mentions. This is a primary reason for why simply experimenting with a social media account is not likely to bear much fruit.

Effective social media requires a steady time investment and a commitment to continue working until you realize your goals. Building a social network is not something that happens overnight.

BOTTOM LINE

Measuring reach may be the route to a solid benchmark of a library's efforts in social media. Keep in mind that this measurement will likely mean the most in the long term.

NOTES

1. John D. Sutter, "Ashton Kutcher Challenges CNN to Twitter Popularity Contest," 2009, www.cnn.com/2009/TECH/04/15/ashton.cnn.twitter.battle/index.html.

2. Clive Thompson, "Clive Thompson in Praise of Online Obscurity," 2010, www.wired.com/magazine/2010/01/st_thompson_obscurity.

3. Ibid.

4. Rebecca Atkinson, "How to Measure Reach and Quantify Your Social Media Campaigns—Part One," 2008, http://thedirectapproach.ca/2008/11/how-to-measure-reach-and-quantify-your-social-media-campaigns-part-one/.

6
IS IT WORTH IT?

Above all, don't engage in social media
if you aren't prepared to change in the bargain.

—JOSHUA-MICHÉLE ROSS, SENIOR VICE PRESIDENT
OF DIGITAL STRATEGY, FLEISHMAN HILLARD

In the end, the question your library administrators will ask is, Is it worth it? No one answer will fit every library, because the goals will differ from one library to the next. Expectations of your administrators will also probably differ. Some may consider the value of actual interactions with members of their community to be invaluable regardless of the metrics. Gathering the opinions of people in your library's community and growing a network of potential advocates has its own intrinsic value that might not be adequately measured with numbers. This is why knowing what your goals are ahead of time will help to answer this question: Is social media worth it for our library? If your library is meeting its stated social media–related objectives, then the answer to the question is probably yes.

BOTTOM LINE
Each library will have to determine its method of figuring ROI,
just as each has to decide what its social media goals are.
Once the method has been determined, use it consistently to
figure out if social media is paying off for your library.

WHAT IF IT'S NOT WORKING?

It's incredibly easy to get wrapped up in the initial enthusiasm for social media. At some point, however, reality is going to settle in and you may find that your hopes don't match the reality. Now what? Do you automatically pull the plug?

How Do You Know If You're Actually Failing?

The first question to ask in this situation is, How do we recognize failure? Just as with everything else concerning social media, the answer to this is not the same for every library. A situation considered to be a failure by one library might be considered a success by another. Again, to know whether or not your library's involvement in social media has been a success will mean coming back to its original objectives and goals.

The first thing to do when deciding if any project has failed is to look at the original parameters given to the project. Were the goals realistic and stated accurately? Was the project planned well? If the intent was for your library to gain hundreds of followers in just a couple of months on a given site, this may be the cause of your discontent: it probably wasn't a realistic deliverable. As we already know, building social networks is a long-term effort that doesn't usually have instant outcomes. If your library's new YouTube video didn't go viral with thousands of views, this shouldn't be a total surprise. Only a very small percentage of the thousands of videos created daily ever make viral status. Make sure that your library's expectations were sensible to begin with.

Reasons That Social Media Efforts Fail

Even if your library's original plan was realistic and had an accurate time frame, your social media endeavors still may not be up to expectations. There are several common problems organizations encounter that can hinder them in the social media space.

Using the Wrong Channel

Did your library create a profile on MySpace, only to learn that most of its patrons use Facebook? Or, did the library create its own social network on a tool like Ning, which has a much more niche audience? If you're not seeing the number of social connections you want to have, it's time to go back and do more research. If you haven't already, survey your library's patrons to see what social media sites they use the most. What you find may surprise you. It could be the majority of your patrons aren't even using social media yet, and that social media may not be the best outreach method for your library at this point.

Using the Wrong People

Just because the reference librarian already had a Facebook profile doesn't necessarily mean he understands how to engage patrons or speak for the library in social media. Likewise, just because the PR person knows how to market with print materials doesn't mean she's qualified to handle social media, either. It takes a certain mind-set and a certain type of expertise to do social media well. It's important to remember that the best person in your library for the job may not be the one you would normally assign to do something like this. Doing social media successfully for your library is not about a staff member's seniority or position, it's about what will work best for the library.

Creating Poor Content

If your library has been making the common mistake of primarily using social media as a marketing platform for its collections and programs, then its content probably lacks interest or relevance to the majority of its followers. One of the things that makes content successful is making sure there is a "hook" to capture readers' attention. Interesting content will generally be humorous, useful, or newsworthy. Take care to ensure that whatever is being posted is not only useful but also entertaining.

Lack of Content

Part of establishing any relationship is steady contact. Your library needs to post very regularly. If your social media posts only happen a couple of times per week, this is not enough to build on, especially in a medium where twenty-four hours is an exceptionally long amount of time to go without any communication. Ensure you're participating daily at the absolute minimum.

Lack of Trust

In order for your fans to engage with your library online, there has to be an established sense of trust. Trust is built in many ways in social media. While it might seem easy to trust a library, that's not always the case. Make sure your library's social media profiles are filled out completely and that any avatars being displayed are professional and easy to understand. Again, another component of trust is responsiveness. Did your library wait too long to respond to comments or mentions? Or did it fail to respond at all to a compliment or a complaint? Each time a patron has to wait overly long for a response, chances are good that person will decide the library isn't online to engage in conversation and trust is lost.

Lack of Buy-in

In chapter 1, I pointed out how important administrative buy-in is to social media for getting the end results you want. Without buy-in, you may not have enough time and commitment to implement your library's social media effort effectively. Other issues can arise as well, such as misunderstandings about the purpose of social media or what it can accomplish. However, a lack of administrative support is not the only kind of deficiency in this area; a lack of support from other staff can be just as problematic. No social media coordinator wants to hear this kind of comment: Why are we doing that stupid Twitter thing when we have patrons waiting at the reference desk? These uninformed comments from staff can drain any enthusiasm for the project and ultimately undermine its effectiveness. Even if you succeeded in getting the backing of the library's director or board, there needs to be a sufficient sense of ownership from staff members as well. Being able to identify a lack of commitment (or hostility in its various forms) to social media will go a long way toward resolving issues with those who are directly or indirectly contributing to failed objectives.

Inability to Change

Joshua-Michéle Ross is senior vice president of digital strategy with Fleishman Hillard and an O'Reilly Radar blogger. He writes: "When an organization makes an investment in social media it is a constructive opportunity to consider not only what could go wrong, but why it could go wrong. In other words, what are the valid criticisms that customers and employees might have and what you are willing to do about it. If you aren't willing to consider the former and have no power concerning the latter, social media might not be your best bet."[1] Ross points out that those organizations that are doing social media well understand that goals and methods will likely change, even incrementally, as part of their participation. If your library is not prepared to accept recommendations for change from third parties, social media is a difficult medium to be in.

Fear

Fear may be the most common obstacle for any organization as it begins to interact in the social media space. Social media is a new venue, and anything new often generates apprehension. Combine fear of the new with the fact that all of the guidelines for interaction and evaluation are also new (making some metrics suspect), and you can end up with the sense that social media is really too new to, well, even try.

Effective social media often means an organization may have to undergo something of a cultural shift, at least in its mind-set. Oft-touted factors such as transparency, authenticity, and honesty are quickly becoming clichés, but the fact is they still matter. The library's online community is going to want to know what's going on at the library, both the good and the bad.

Make an honest assessment about how your library is interacting in social media. Are responses to questions or comments made from a foundation of fear, honesty, or both? Is the library only connecting to others it considers somehow "safe," such as other libraries or organizations? Is the library sticking to only its usual content, such as links to the catalog or programs? If you find that these behaviors are a regular part of the library's social media interactions, it's time to acknowledge they are rooted in fear. Until the library can overcome that fear, it's not likely social media is going to be a productive medium for it.

BOTTOM LINE

You need to revisit your goals first to know if social media isn't working for your library. Make sure that your library isn't having issues with problematic behaviors, people, or content before deciding to pull the plug. Be prepared to be flexible and to listen. Just as the online community is an open forum, giving staff a chance to feel they are part of the process and that you care about their concerns may be enough to blunt criticism and resistance.

WHEN DO YOU PULL THE PLUG?

As with every new program a library undertakes, there is always a chance it may not turn out as expected. Some endeavors succeed, some fail. If you feel social media or a particular social media site has not panned out for your library, here are some steps you should take to ensure you have covered all of your bases.

1. **You've removed all misunderstandings, failure behaviors, and impractical expectations.** You've already tweaked your strategies and managed any other issues mentioned previously, so you know your goals are within reason and not being hindered by other factors. Then you tried again over a period of time and evaluated the results one way or the other; in other words, you know you've tried absolutely everything to be successful.

2. **You've done the objective evaluation of the library's social media presence and interactions.** The results of your metrics or evaluative questions clearly show that there is little or no ROI despite your best efforts.

3. **You may already have a lot of resources invested — make doubly sure it's a failure before deciding to opt out.** Don't let subjective or emotional responses factor into your decision-making process. You also may have built up social capital already that may be difficult to recover at a later time.

4. **You've enlisted the aid of others within the scope and parameters of your library's policies without success.** Sometimes, all it takes is one person from outside to notice a crucial element or offer a critical piece of input or idea to help set you on the right track. Remember, establishing your library's presence in social media won't be accomplished without careful planning and the contributions of many people.

BOTTOM LINE

You need to ensure that your library did everything it could to succeed before deciding social media didn't work this time around.

HOW TO PULL THE PLUG

Pulling the plug is part of a natural process. Not every project will succeed; this is a risk of trying something new. Recognize this reality up front and try to avoid becoming too personally attached to the project. Once the decision has been made to stop participating in social media, either partially or wholly, be prepared to follow through.

TABLE 6.1 **The Do's and Don't's of Pulling the Plug**

DO	DON'T
■ Be honest. Explain what caused the decision to stop tweeting, posting, etc.	■ Abandon the account and just stop tweeting, posting, etc., with no explanation.
■ Give people an alternative place to connect with the library. For example, if you're leaving MySpace, give them the link to your Facebook profile.	■ Tell people to visit the library on its website if there's no way to communicate there beyond a basic contact form. People who connected with your library in one medium (social media) will not likely switch to another that uses only one-way communication.
■ Accept that not everyone is going to be happy about this. Sympathize and respond to individuals if you can and be ready to explain the decision.	■ Try to please every squeaky wheel who complains.
■ Keep the account open (do not confuse an open account with posting on it). Never give up control of a profile with your library's name on it. Even if it is not in use, it prevents brandjacking.	■ Close the account entirely, making it possible for someone to take the library's namespace on that social network.
■ Leave a final message explaining why nothing new is happening with the profile.	■ Leave the account inactive with no final message to explain why there is no new content.

Probably the most difficult aspect of leaving social media is letting go of the connections you have built up. Your library created a profile and people connected to it with an expectation of regular communication. The question then becomes: How do we just stop communicating with these people who trusted us enough to connect? This is a hard choice to make. Table 6.1 offers some dos and don'ts to make the process a little easier.

BOTTOM LINE

*Be firm, but honest, about explaining the decision
to stop participating in a particular network. Be clear about
where the library will be online going forward.*

NOTE

1. Joshua-Michéle Ross, "Why Social Media Isn't for Everyone," 2010,
   http://mashable.com/2010/01/18/social-media-not-for-everyone/.

A FEW FINAL WORDS

The days of shouting and imposing your message on the masses are gone.

—ERIK QUALMAN, AUTHOR OF *SOCIALNOMICS*

Social media is a long-term process of building relationships with individuals, rather than any kind of marketing to the masses. This is the core of what makes social media different from traditional media. When your library is tweeting on Twitter, posting Facebook status updates, uploading YouTube videos, or doing whatever comes next in social media, it's all about building those relationships. It's not really about how many followers or fans or views. It's not even so much about branding. It's about creating personalized connections that actually allow dialogue between the library as an institution and its patrons. Regularly conversing with people online can allow them to learn more about the library, and allow the library to learn more about what people want from it.

Social media can allow your library to create goodwill and direct connections. Not just direct connections within its community, but also connections to a *wider* community that can get the word out when a crisis might arise (as in the case of the Save Ohio Libraries campaign). Social media is the new, faster, and more widespread word of mouth, and it behooves a library to have a place in these communities and participate in the dialogue. In no small way, it's a lot like the old expression, "If you don't make a decision, one will be made for you." In the case of social media, that decision will likely be made without your consent, knowledge, or input.

What is the bottom line for libraries? At the end of the day, social media is all about *people* and *relationships* with them. To believe otherwise is to waste time and effort. Be human. Spend time listening and talking to others rather than merely pushing out various forms of advertising. Social media is a new way to engage with patrons. Keep that in mind as you go forward and do social media. Do it so it matters.

BIBLIOGRAPHY

Atkinson, Rebecca. "How to Measure Reach and Quantify Your Social Media Campaigns—Part Two." http://thedirectapproach.ca/2008/11/how-to-measure-reach-and-quantify-your-social-media-campaigns-part-two/.

_____. "How to Measure Reach and Quantify Your Social Media Campaigns—Part Three." http://thedirectapproach.ca/2008/11/how-to-measure-reach-and-quantify-your-social-media-campaigns-part-three/.

_____. "Quantify Your Non-Profit's Social Media ROI." 2008. http://johnhaydon.com/2008/11/quantify-your-social-media-campaigns/.

Balwani, Samir. "5 Advanced Social Media Marketing Strategies for Small Businesses." 2009. http://mashable.com/2009/09/30/small-business-strategies/.

_____. "5 Simple Things Most Social Media Marketers Forget to Do." 2009. http://samirbalwani.com/social-media-marketing/5-simple-things-most-social-media-marketers-forget-to-do/.

_____. "Don't Rush into Social Marketing, Think about It First." 2009. http://samirbalwani.com/social-media-marketing/dont-rush-into-social-media-marketing/.

Barone, Lisa. "Creating Your Social Media Plan." 2009. http://outspokenmedia.com/social-media/social-media-planning/.

Bennett, Shéa. "Why Everybody Needs a Follow Policy on Twitter." 2009. http://twittercism.com/follow-policy/.

Blanchard, Olivier. "Olivier Blanchard Basics of Social Media ROI." 2009. www.slideshare.net/thebrandbuilder/olivier-blanchard-basics-of-social-media-roi/.

Boches, Edward. "Four Mistakes You Could Make in Social Media." 2009. http://edwardboches.com/four-mistakes-you-could-make-in-social-media/.

Brogan, Chris. "Get on the Right Side of the Fence." 2009. www.chrisbrogan.com/get-on-the-right-side-of-the-fence/.

_____. "Prioritize Your Social Media Efforts." 2009. www.chrisbrogan.com/prioritize-your-social-media-efforts/.

Bullas, Jeff. "Social Media Survey Reveals 92% of Companies Using Social Media." 2009. http://jeffbullas.com/2009/11/16/social-media-survey-reveals-92-of-companies-using-social-media/.

Burkhardt, Andrew. "Seven More Things Libraries Should Tweet." 2009. http://andyburkhardt.com/2009/10/19/seven-more-things-libraries-should-tweet/.

Catone, Josh. "Before You Go Online: Talk to Your Customers Offline." 2009. http://mashable.com/2009/11/17/small-business-customers/.

Collier, Mack. "This is why the 'authority matters' argument is total BS." 2008. http://moblogsmoproblems.blogspot.com/2008/12/this-is-why-authority-matters-argument.html.

Connor, Angela. "Six Ways to Get Social Media Buy-in from the Boss." 2008. http://blog.angelaconnor.com/2008/11/23/sixways-to-get-social-media-buy-in-from-the-boss/.

Cottingham, Rob. "Cartoon: Head Count." 2009. www.readwriteweb.com/archives/cartoon_head_count.php.

Dvorak, John C. "Nine Ways to Use Twitter." 2009. www.pcmag.com/article2/0,2817,2343672,00.asp.

eMarketer. "Why You Need a Strategy for Social Media." 2010. www.emarketer.com/Article.aspx?R=1007508/.

Evans, Meryl K. "32 Ways to Use Facebook for Business." 2009. http://webworkerdaily.com/2009/07/21/32-ways-to-use-facebook-for-business/.

Ferenstein, Greg. "The Science of Building Trust with Social Media." 2010. http://mashable. com/2010/02/24/social-media-trust/.

Finn, Greg. "What Results Can I Expect from My Social Media Campaign?" 2009. http://searchengineland.com/what-results-can-i-expect-from-my-social-media-campaign-16355/.

Fitton, Laura. "Selling Social Media 'Up' to Management." 2008. http://pistachioconsulting. com/selling-social-media-up-to-management/.

Francois, Laurent. "Sentiment analysis crap in social media." 2009. www.socialmediatoday.com/SMC/121398/.

Gordhamer, Soren. "5 Ways Social Media Is Changing Our Daily Lives." 2009. http://mashable. com/2009/10/16/social-media-changing-lives/.

_____. "When Do You Use Twitter Versus Facebook?" 2009. http://mashable.com/2009/08/01/facebook-vs-twitter/.

Hunt, Tara. *The Whuffie Factor: Using the Power of Social Networks to Build Your Business.* New York, NY: Crown Business, 2009.

Kroski, Ellyssa. "Should Your Library Have a Social Media Policy?" 2009. www.schoollibraryjournal. com/article/CA6699104.html.

Lacy, Kyle. "5 Ways to Help Face the Fear of Social Media." 2009. http://kylelacy.com/5-ways-to-help-face-the-fear-of-social-media/.

_____. "10 Ways to Build Trust with Social Media." 2009. http://kylelacy.com/10-ways-to-build-trust-with-social-media/.

Laidlaw, Georgina. "Get Better Connected on Social Networks." 2010. http://webworkerdaily. com/2010/02/14/get-better-connected-on-social-networks/.

Lauby, Sharlyn. "5 Ways to Make Your Business More Transparent." 2009. http://mashable. com/2009/09/30/business-transparency/.

Low, Roderick. "It's Not the Steps, It's the Connection." 2009. www.penn-olson.com/2009/12/23/social-media-its-not-the-steps-its-the-connection/.

MacManus, Richard. "40% of People 'Friend' Brands on Facebook." 2009. www.readwriteweb.com/archives/survey_brands_making_big_impact_on_facebook_twitter.php.

McConnell, Ben. "The Last Temptation of Twitter." 2008. www.churchofcustomer.com/2008/12/an-8020-rule-for-selfpromotion.html.

Malicoat, Todd. "7 Reasons Your Social Media Marketing Failed (and how to fix it!)." 2009. www. stuntdubl.com/2009/01/12/social-marketing-failure/.

Merrill, Mike. "Why Every Employee Is a Salesperson—The Power of Social Media." 2009. http://mikemerrill.com/wordpress/2009/07/why-every-employee-is-a-salesperson-the-power-of-social-media/.

Notter, Jamie. "Is Your Organization Human Enough for Social Media?" 2009. www.socialfish. org/2009/11/human-enough.html.

Ostrow, Adam. "Half of Social Media Users Connect with Brands." 2009. http://mashable. com/2009/08/31/social-media-brands/.

Pigott, Ike. "How to Be a Social Media Advocate in Conservative Corporate Cultures." 2009. www. slideshare.net/ikepigott/how-to-be-a-social-media-advocate-in/.

Pingdom.com. Study: Males vs. females in social networks. 2009. http://royal.pingdom. com/2009/11/27/study-males-vs-females-in-social-networks/.

_____. Study: Ages of social network users. 2010. http://royal.pingdom.com/2010/02/16/study-ages-of-social-network-users/.

Porterfield, Amy. "The 'Cool Kids' Strategy to Social Media Marketing." 2009. http://amyporterfield. com/index.php/2009/11/the-cool-kids-strategy-to-social-media-marketing/.

Qualman, Erik. *Socialnomics: How Social Media Transforms the Way We Live and Do Business.* Hoboken, NJ: John Wiley & Sons, Inc., 2009.

Randall, Kim. "How You Use Social Media Says a Lot about You and Your Brand." 2009. www. kimrandall.me/how-you-use-social-media-says-a-lot-about-you-and-your-brand/.

Robbins, Renee. "7 Creative Ways to Introduce Social Media to Your Team." 2009. http://learningputty. com/2009/10/22/7-creative-ways-to-introduce-social-media-to-your-team/.

Rogers-Urbanek, Jenica P. "Going Beyond the Great Idea: Getting buy-in and doing effective training for 2.0 projects." 2008. www2.potsdam.edu/rogersjp/CiL2008Acad2.0.pdf

Ross, Joshua-Michéle. "Why Social Media Isn't for Everyone." 2010. http://mashable.com/2010/01/18/social-media-not-for-everyone/.

Schaefer, Mark W. "How Social Media Can Hurt Business Relationships." 2009. http://businessesgrow.com/2009/12/20/how-social-media-can-hurt-business-relationships/.

Schawbel, Dan. "HOW TO: Build Your Personal Brand on Twitter." 2009. http://mashable.com/2009/05/20/twitter-personal-brand/.

Sherman, Aliza. "The Reluctant Social Media Client." 2008. http://webworkerdaily.com/2008/11/21/the-reluctant-social-media-client/.

_____. "6 Tips for Better Branding Using Avatars." 2009. http://webworkerdaily.com/2009/07/16/6-tips-for-better-branding-using-avatars/.

_____. "The Value of Twitter Followers: Quality Over Quantity." 2009. http://webworkerdaily.com/2009/07/02/the-value-of-twitter-followers-quality-over-quantity/.

_____. "Why Should I Engage in Social Media?" 2009. http://webworkerdaily.com/2009/09/28/why-should-i-engage-in-social-media-for-business/.

Smith, Mari. "Social Media Success—15 Hot Tips from the Pied Piper!" 2009. www.marismith.com/social-media-success-15-hot-tips-from-the-pied-piper/.

Solis, Brian. "What IF We Redefined Influence? The New Influence Factor in Social Media." 2009. www.briansolis.com/2009/11/what-if-we-redefined-influence-the-evolution-of-the-influence-factor-in-social-media/?success/.

_____. "The Maturation of Social Media ROI." 2010. http://mashable.com/2010/01/26/maturation-social-media-roi/.

Spiro, Josh. "A New Source of Stress: Feelings of Social Media Inadequacy." 2009. www.inc.com/news/articles/2009/12/afraid-of-social-media.html.

Strickland, Marta. "How to Do Social Media Right in 2009." 2009. www.slideshare.net/mstrickland/how-to-do-social-media-right-in-2009/

Sukernek, Warren. "@HiltonAnaheim—There's more to Twitter than broadcasting your ads." 2009. http://twittermaven.blogspot.com/2009/12/hiltonanaheim-theres-more-to-twitter.html.

Sutter, John D. "Ashton Kutcher Challenges CNN to Twitter Popularity Contest." 2009. www.cnn.com/2009/TECH/04/15/ashton.cnn.twitter.battle/index.html.

Sutton, Wayne. "7 Habits of Highly Effective Twitterers." 2009. http://blog.mrtweet.com/7-habits-of-highly-effective-twitterers-wayne-sutton/.

Thompson, Clive. "Clive Thompson in Praise of Online Obscurity." 2010. www.wired.com/magazine/2010/01/st_thompson_obscurity/.

Twittown. "Five Wickedly Clever Ways to Use Twitter." 2009. http://twittown.com/social-networks/social-networks-blog/five-wickedly-clever-ways-use-twitter/.

Uhrmacher, Aaron. "How to Measure Social Media ROI for Business." 2008. http://mashable.com/2008/07/31/measuring-social-media-roi-for-business/.

Van Grove, Jennifer. "19% of Internet Users Now Use Status Updates." 2009. http://mashable.com/2009/10/21/pew-september-data/.

_____. "What Social Media Users Want." 2010. http://mashable.com/2010/03/18/social-media-sites-data/.

Warren, Christina. "HOW TO: Measure Social Media ROI." 2009. http://mashable.com/2009/10/27/social-media-roi/.

Website Monitoring Blog. Facebook Facts & Figures (history & statistics). 2010. www.website-monitoring.com/blog/2010/03/17/facebook-facts-and-figures-history-statistics/.

Williams, Alex. "Study: Enterprise Lags in Social Web Savviness." 2009. www.readwriteweb.com/enterprise/2009/10/deloitte-study-shows-the-enter.php.

Worthington, Paul. "How to Be Generous: A Guide for Social Media Brands." 2009. http://mashable.com/2009/06/18/social-media-generosity/.

INDEX

You may also be interested in

Building a Buzz: Libraries and Word-of-Mouth Marketing: Two creative marketers, Peggy Barber and Linda Wallace, bring you sound marketing principles to spread the word about your library within the community with a strategy that works for you, WOMM must-haves, tips to effectively deliver your message, best practices and insightful reviews, and much more.

Marketing Public Libraries eCourse: This self-paced tutorial explains how to create effective, community-based marketing campaigns using the latest and most popular Web 2.0 tools. Quizzes at the end of each lesson test your knowledge, while Further Reading suggestions point you in the direction of additional information.

I Found It on the Internet: Coming of Age Online, **Second Edition:** Texting, tweeting, chatting, blogging, and other social networking largely occur in a free-for-all environment of unbridled access; quality takes a backseat to quantity. To help librarians, educators, and parents step in to guide teens' decision making, Frances Jacobson Harris offers a thoroughly updated edition of her classic book.

Inside, Outside, and Online: Building Your Library Community: Based on a scan of the community and technology environments that libraries operate within, the related literature, and the practical experiences of hundreds of library staff actively building communities through their work, this book provides much-needed insights into the essential elements of community building.

Order today at www.alastore.ala.org or 866-746-7252!

ALA Store purchases fund advocacy, awareness, and accreditation programs for library professionals worldwide.